DEDICATED TO:

INDICA AND CHAVA

THEY TAUGHT ME SO MUCH

CHAPTERS

ACKNOWLEDGEMENTS

There are so many people that deserve recognition. The first of which would be my daughter Treya for giving me purpose and for proving to me that if I never do anything else, that I will have done at least 1 great thing. My wife Shawna for her unwavering love and support and for being the best thing that has ever happened to me that I didn't help build. My son Draven for granting me long held wishes and validating that the future is in good hands. My grandmother Jeanne for her constant encouragement, inspiration and for teaching me that blood may be thicker than water but it is much thinner than love. My grandfather Robert Ross, for being the man that I hope that I become because of his honesty, stern resolution and the love that I always saw in his eyes. I would also like to thank Ron James and Tom Davy for instilling in me the work ethic, love of life and family that I have today, regardless of relation. These two men were what served as my father figures and I wouldn't be the man I am without them. I would be remiss not to thank my sister Leslie for showing me, by example, what dedication and perseverance means. My brother Jared for being the kind of guy that you can't ever be around enough. I thank my Hyper-intelligent, genuinely thought provoking and hilarious cousin Josh for his essential insights and help during the editing process. I want to thank Jeremy for being such a great friend since our fight on the playground in the 4th grade and for being, probably the best person that I will ever meet. I can't forget Toby Caudill for giving me answers and even more questions or Jay Nabb for being a super human friend, builder and father. I would never forget my, brother from another mother; Ivan, for getting me out on the road and helping to change my perception, and for being a part of some of the most enlightening conversations, life-altering experiences and unforgettable times of my life! And, of course, Jen, the most refreshingly crazy part of my crazy life and for always being there at the right times, oh, and for the pizza;) I need to thank Valiant for showing me a better path as a youngster and Wookiefoot for the soundtrack, make believe and much needed direction for my journey. This section would be longer than this book if I gave the necessary appreciation to each of these people or if I thanked everyone in my life that has helped to make me who I am today. Those of you not listed know who you are and know that I love you. Thank all of you so very much, I wouldn't be me without you!!!

PLEDGE

I pledge allegiance to the world,
and to all the good people that share it with me,
and to all that is right,
for which they stand,
all nations, bound by love, indivisible,
with aspirations of prosperity for all.

FOREWORD

Ok, I'm guessing that the title made you want to read this book for one reason or another. Well good, that was the plan. I don't care whether you are reading it because you are appalled by the title and want more ammo for your twitter tirades or because you have been thinking the same thing and crave validation. Either way, you are both reading it. No matter how much you disagree, you agreed to read this book which in itself lends a little insight into what this book is about.

My hope in writing this is to show that you are both wrong..... and right, and also to start a conversation that you and I can continue to learn from. If you think that you have a plan to fix everything for good, you're wrong. The problems are always changing and our plans are going to have to evolve as well to keep pace. This is a simple mathematic principle; you can't add or subtract something from something and have the same thing. This works with numbers, people, environments and anything else you can think of. Thinking that the variables could continue to change and our ways of dealing with them stay the same is lunacy, and the want to do so is driven by stubbornness and ego (and sometimes money). If we are not ok with having and needing to continuously learn and grow to deal with these issues then we are doomed to a life of self-inflicted ignorance. This only perpetuates the cycle because that is how most of the issues became issues in the first place.

One of the things that keeps people from getting on the same page is separation, in its innumerous forms, and some of these will be covered in the chapters ahead. We do it to ourselves and it is often done for or to us, but it (separation), is always chosen by someone or something. Even when it is a consequence of choosing to not separate yourself from something else. This is not to say that separation is a bad thing, and that is also something that I hope to show you in the pages ahead. You've made it this far without throwing this book in the trash and I encourage you to resist that urge, as strong as it may be at times, and to power through to the end. Whether I have brought up something that you hadn't previously seen in that light or you think that I am batshit crazy I still impel you to finish reading. Even if it is just to add to the list of the many reasons that you think that I am batshit crazy, keep reading. I look forward to the feedback, it is the reason that I am doing this. I do not profess to know it all, I barely know a little bit of some, but I am keeping an open mind and an even more open heart in my search for any knowledge that can help me grow along the way. That is where you come in. These are just thoughts and ideas that I have been introduced to or come up with myself over the years and only with the knowledge that I've garnered.

I most certainly do have my own opinions, as do you, and I don't expect us to agree on all of them. I also know that my opinions can change if given worthy cause for such an effect. I hope that yours can do the same and I want to hear them just in case they are able to change mine. I want you to shoot holes in my theories, tell me what you agree with or what you might have if I had added another piece of information. Tell me that I had it all wrong and the reasons why, that's great! I want you and the knowledge that you have compiled to come to this party too! The conversation and swapping of ideas is exactly what I'm after. It's the only way we are going to be able to make any plans to make this world a better place. Compassionate, thoughtful and understanding debate along with a healthy dose of compromise are the only ways that we are going to truly fix anything.

 Some people say not to sweat the small stuff but I spend my time doing quite the opposite. A few years ago, I was devoured by the photography bug and one of my favorite types is macro photography (funny that I am usually taking pictures of bugs). In doing so, my eyes were opened to an intricate and mesmerizing world that I had taken for granted by not sweating the small stuff. There are countless droves of surprises behind every pile of pollen or reflection in a dragonfly's wings and the same can be said for life without the need for magnification. Nevertheless, there is no such thing as a big thing. Even the largest thing that you can manage to muster the thought of is made up of a plethora of little things. We used to think that grains of sand were what everything was made of. Then we found the atom, and then that was the smallest thing that we knew of…. until we split that to shed light on the world of protons, neutrons and electrons. We thought those were the smallest things until we found that each of these are made up of three quarks. Even though we have gotten to a point with quarks that we don't know how to split them, we still don't know that there aren't smaller objects still to be discovered. Our ability to see smaller will have to grow before we can answer these questions, which judging from the past, will only grow in number as well. So, if there is no such thing as a big thing and everything is made up of smaller things, then what sense does not sweating anything make?

I look forward to the journey that this book has laid before us, and to talking to and meeting with the different people that will be involved in the writing and reading of it. Thank you so much for being a part.

CHOICES AND SEPARATION

First and foremost, you are you, and you have been since before you were born. We all start out as individuals, each different from the one before or any after. The things that happen afterwards, the choices that you make and the decisions that are made for you, will all have a part in who you will become but you are who you are from the beginning and you are different from everyone else. Just like in a litter of puppies, one will love to be held while another won't have it for a second. One will like to chew, one will like to chase. Another will run straight into the unknown while another is afraid of its own shadow. Still another can't be bothered to get out of bed. All of these puppies had the same mother and father, they weren't corrupted by television or video games and they got the same education but all managed to be different. I don't believe that there is a thing in this world that isn't different. Similar yes, but not exactly the same. This is precisely what makes life so fantastically interesting and eminently precious. Being a young boy and noticing this fact made it hard for me to ever take a racist seriously. There is obviously a lack of intelligence and an overabundance of ignorance present in them and I tend to distance myself from such elements that refuse to listen or learn. I'm fine with that form of separation in this case.

 We make choices every day that help to define us. Whether we like it or not, some of these choices separate us from other parts of society. We make some of these choices to intentionally separate ourselves (division) while others are made without the intent but with the same end result (separation). At the same time some are made for us by things that are out of our control such as our parents, teachers and even our physical location. Every decision we make, or that is made for us, from religion, to music preference, clothing, jobs and even hobbies, among many others, do their part to define who we are but also to define who we are not. In doing so, we mentally and sometimes physically separate ourselves from people that believe, dress or work in a different way or place.

 One of the decisions that is made for us is physical location. You have no control over where you are born yet this factor will define you more than most. If nothing else, this is true simply because we are only the end result of how we process what we have seen, felt or experienced up to that point. We can't be affected by something that we have not yet encountered in some way shape or form. If it, or its influence, can't be found in your proximity you can't be affected by it. You will however be affected by those things that are in your proximity and every single piece of that input changes who you are.

Nothing in this world is exactly the same or ever will be. Every blade of grass, leaf of a tree and every drop of water, even every galaxy or speck of space dust is different. How can we not expect people to follow this all-encompassing rule? You aren't even the same person that you were yesterday and won't be the same tomorrow. We are constantly absorbing, learning and growing. That is change, and it is the only truly constant and consistent thing that I can think of. Even a carbon copy or clone has many minute physical differences from the original. Even if they appear to be exactly alike, they are still occupying a different physical space and are being affected differently by varying conditions (light, wind, thought, etc.).

Think of it like a photograph. If two people stand side by side and take a picture of the same object at the same time, the pictures may look similar but cannot be exactly the same because they were taken from different angles. This is the case, simply because two people cannot occupy the same space. Therefore, the object will be viewed differently because of the angle of perception, the angle of the light source or even any dust particles in the air, just to name a few of the many variables. Even if one person took a picture and then moved out of the way and then the other person moved in and managed to get their camera in the exact same position (highly unlikely), the pictures would be different because of even the smallest change of any of the previously cited conditions (not to mention each cameras' intricacies). Even if it were in a vacuum and all of those conditions weren't a factor, the pictures would be taken at two different times making them, by definition, different. The second picture is not of the same object but of that object when it is older.

These are just the technical differences in the picture, but what about perception? The mood, idea or thoughts provoked by the image will be perceived differently by different people because people are different regardless of input (everything is). These perceptions are all changed by how the individual processed their surroundings and the other information that they have encountered prior.

When brought up by the same parents, belief system, schools, etc. some people will conform to all of these things while others will conform to none and every variation in between. People are different and process the very same data in very different ways because of it. Compound that by seeing things from a different angle or space, along with data coming in from different sources (who got their information from a myriad of sources) that the other person doesn't have contact with and it starts to become clearer how views/perceptions can differ so greatly.

 I think that it's funny that there are people that refuse to accept that change is inevitable while others feel the need to change things just for the sake of change. I'm a huge proponent of, if it ain't broke don't fix it, but if there's a truly better way to do something then the logical side of me doesn't have a problem embracing change. The original telephone wasn't broken. It worked, but I'm betting that you are happier with the version that you have now. I am.

 Change is inevitable, and we need to do our best to adapt to change that we have no control over and deal with it in an understanding and compassionate way. We need to deal with the changes that we do have control of in the same way. You can't catch everything or think of all of the possible outcomes of every situation but I guarantee that if you don't think about it, then you won't think of any of them.

 Thinking about a problem or situation is the first step in deciding how to deal with it, as well as realizing the changes that you'll be making. Thinking about it in an understanding and compassionate way, however, will allow you to make a less selfish and more informed decision. Hopefully this will lessen the chance that you are excluding yourself from something that may benefit you or that you may be able to contribute to. Just as well, from including yourself in something that might not be a benefit to you or that you may be a detriment to. As I said before, you can't catch everything, but a little bit of thought goes a long way. More thought goes even further.

Even well thought out, innocent decisions make changes that knowingly or unknowingly separate us from other people. Let's say there are two boys that do not know each other, Billy and Johnny. Billy decides early in school that he loves wrestling while Johnny decides that he loves baseball. If they both end up devoting their time and energy solely to bettering themselves at their particular sport for years to come, they are making choices that will separate them. Not because they don't necessarily like the other person or activity but because they chose to play the other sport. Now, because Billy chose wrestling, he spends his time at wrestling practice, he talks about wrestling, travels with the wrestling team and probably hangs out with someone from the team simply because of common interests and sheer proximity. All the while Johnny is doing the same thing except that everything is baseball to him. Billy and Johnny probably don't hang out much. Even if they do, the decisions that they made put them around many other influences. It also took time from building friendships outside of the activity and placed them around people that may now fill that role because of new found interest, or just because they were around more often.

We make these choices even with the way we dress, whether it is because of a societal norm, fad, the refusal to be a part of one or out of sheer necessity. The jock, prep, stoner, business man, construction worker and hippy all dress differently and separate themselves in the process. If you gauge your ears, wear skinny jeans and grow a beard to offset your man bun then you won't stand out that much at a Starbucks. The same could probably not be said for a board meeting for a fortune 500 company. Not to say that those two things can't get along, but it sure won't be hard to pick you out of the crowd.

This is the problem that most people have. They focus more on the differences than they do the similarities. I have been a victim of it myself on more than one occasion. I have met a few of those hipster looking clones that were way more business on the inside than some of the monkey suit wearing cityots I've met. You may meet someone that doesn't at all look the part of someone that you would normally hangout with. But, after spending some time with them, you find that they are your kindred spirit that you couldn't imagine the rest of your life without. If you focus only on the differences, you may never have the chance to meet that person. This is why I try to save the brunt of my judgement until I have seen enough data to make a more educated decision.

That doesn't mean that when I see a shark that I'm going to stay in the water until I see aggressive actions. I am definitely getting back in the boat a.s.a.p.! But in this case, the shark just being in the water is enough of an action for me to judge that it needs more space, and far be it from me to deny it of that, so back in the boat I go:) I am not saying that the shark had any intentions of biting me. My judgement wasn't based on the fact that it would bite me, but just the fact that it could. I would take myself out of the mix just to make sure.

The wrong answer, I believe, is to hold the shark responsible for the "might", maybe or even a real bite or kill. I put myself in its domain, what should I expect? I should remove myself from the equation and leave the shark to live its life and do its job. It is, after all, the shark's house and I can't imagine that it would last too long if I came home to find it in mine. By removing myself from the equation by not even getting in the water at all, my chances of being bitten by a shark are 0%. Step foot in the water and the chances increase dramatically. By not getting in, the chances of enjoying my time in the ocean also go down to 0%. I'm 100% ok with those figures but you are going to need to do your own math.

It isn't your right to be able to enjoy time in its house whenever you please any more than it is its right to hang out at your house. Maybe you'd be ok with the shark coming over and hanging out for a little while. But how happy will you be when it brings all of its family and friends and they bring theirs and everybody trashes the place regularly? What if they brought vessels to haul all of your food away and just started picking off your friends and family as if they were trying to eradicate your species? You'd want the headlines to say that you are the victim, wouldn't you? That's what I thought. If I were the

8

shark, I'd bite you whether you looked like a food source or not. Your greedy ass deserves it.

We are a headline driven society and don't tend to do more than, maybe, skim through the story, if at all. That is, unless it is shocking enough to peak our interest, but those interests are becoming shockingly harder to peak every day. We believe these headlines as if they are the truth and take a side without doing any research of our own. If the front-page headline reads, "Bob stabbed six puppies" that is what everyone goes away believing. Not nearly as many people see the retraction the next day, on page 8, in small print that says it was a type-o and should have read, "Bob saved sick puppies". So to most, true or not, Bob is a puppy killer.

We go about our day and trade our hard-lined opinions at the water cooler about shit that we couldn't possibly have a clue of due to the many intricate details that we aren't privy to. I don't care whether it is climate change or Bruce/Caitlyn Jenner's sex change, you probably don't have enough knowledge to be an expert on either matter. Unfortunately, we probably have more information from our media about Braitlyn's change than we do about the climate's. This may be by design or it may just be printing what sells, yet again, I don't know. Maybe it's both; they're just the Gucci of misdirection and we just like to buy their designs.

Realizing that you have a problem is the first step towards fixing that problem. You'll hear this in any drug rehab or alcoholics anonymous meeting. It is just as true when applied to the other drugs in our life that can cause problems (thoughts, beliefs, screens, money, etc.). It is hard to admit that you're wrong, mostly if it is because of the way that you were brought up. This would mean that the people that you love, trust and respect were wrong too (or lied). These are hard things to accept but we have to be able to do so because not all parents are right, or right in the head. You can't continue to follow the beliefs that your parents taught you if you believe they aren't true or if you find out they are wrong.

 Let's say Timmy grows up on a sheep farm and his Daddy tells him that they have to fuck the sheep to get them to produce the most wool. Well that's pretty disgusting, but we give Timmy a pass because that's what daddy said, so that's what he believed. When Timmy is finally old enough to go to town with his dad to sell the wool and finds out from the kids and parents from the other sheep farms, that none of them fuck their sheep, it becomes Timmy's choice. If he goes home and beds down with a sheep tonight he isn't doing it because his daddy told him it was the way to be, he's doing it because he likes to fuck sheep. His dad is a sick son-of-a-bitch and should definitely be brought up on charges (of electricity) at the very least, but Timmy is accountable for the continued participation. So, don't blame what you believe on your parents, no matter what twisted story they told you. It was your choice to continue to follow that path, so if you are still metaphorically (I hope) fucking that sheep, it's just because you want to. You nasty mother flocker.

TECHNOLOGY AND ACCOUNTABILITY

 Technology has advanced our society in many ways but I don't know that it has connected us as much as it has separated us from one another. We used to spend a lot of our time outside of our houses doing many things and sometimes just nothing, which gave us more opportunities to get to know our neighbors and others in our community. Knowing people better lets you make better decisions about who to trust and just as importantly, who not to. With the advent of technology such as air conditioning and television the inside of our homes have become much more comfortable and entertaining. This has led to us spending far too much time inside and not developing those relationships with our neighbors and our surroundings. In doing so, we've grown away from each other and stopped trusting each other as much and it is evident in the way that we don't trust others in the community to reprimand our children. I, for one, want the homeowner of the house, that my child just spray-painted, to give them a piece of his mind and bring them by the ear to my house. I would say thank you and take my child and decide on a punishment. The child would then learn that dad is ok with others stopping them from doing wrong and that they will tell his father (or drag him there) and there will be repercussions. Lesson learned. Why wouldn't you want others to look out for you, your children's, or the community's best interest? It does take a village, at least to raise a healthy, well rounded human being.

When the telephone came about, yes it made it easier to get in touch quickly but it also kept you from going to the person's home and having face to face discussions. It is a shame because now we do almost everything we can to avoid face to face interactions. We text, email, call, poke, tweet, and chat and when we're not, we are face down in our screens making sure that we don't look at all accessible to a bystander that may like to start up a conversation. This doesn't even take into account what we are missing by not paying attention to our surroundings. In doing so, we are much less aware of what is really going on.

Now, with as much entertainment that is packed into those little screens we find ourselves lost without that constant stimulation, control and accessibility. You don't have to be a rocket scientist to see the affect that they have on society in general. Just go to a mall or restaurant or take a ride on a train or bus or even across town with your family and take notice of how many people are engulfed by those little screens.

This is not to say that all of these inventions didn't make great advances in other aspects of our lives. On the contrary, they have been hugely instrumental in our "growth" (whether that is a good thing or not is debatable). These pieces of technology can do great things, like saving a life by being able to call 9-1-1 or talking to a relative that would have died before making the trip. It has also made it easier to distribute messages to the public quickly and connect the world to be able to trade information and ideas.

The automobile allowed us to get to work more quickly and to go farther in search of it. In that, and many other ways, it is a great thing but it too has helped to separate us. We don't live as close to our family anymore and we see them and know them less because of it. All of these things can be used for good but when misunderstood, used intentionally for bad or even just ignorantly they can do great harm to the individual and to society as a whole. Take a gun for example, it is a great invention for protection and hunting for food but when people use it for sport killing and other forms of murder it doesn't seem that great.

We as a society have become too accustomed to holding the wrong thing accountable though, and are too quick to blame the gun, car or tv for doing the damage. It is the person in control of the object that is to blame, not the object. It's not the car or the alcohol that is responsible for drunk driving. It is the misuse of both by the operator, not the objects or their manufacturers. If left alone, a gun rarely, if ever, commits a crime. The tv has never held a gun to anyone's head and made them watch. It doesn't matter if it is the person that pulled the trigger, the one that decided to do nothing but sit in front of the tv or the person that keeps trying every trick in the book to keep them interested in the show hoping they'll binge watch another season so their advertisers keep paying them. Each person has a choice to not pull the trigger, to go outside and do something or to just be happy making a decent living providing quality entertainment. They chose to make that tool a weapon. Make sure that your choices are well thought out, informed and steered by equality because you will have to live with them for the rest of your life.

Sometimes we do things with what we feel are the best of intentions but we, and the thing that we do, just get in our way. We program our children and ourselves with attention deficit disorders. With all of the advertisements that tell us that nothing that we are or have is good enough, it is not hard to understand why we bully ourselves or each other for not having the right stuff or looking the right way. It doesn't help that on holidays/birthdays when a child opens up a gift they get to hold it for about ten seconds before they have to put it down to be able to open the next gift. We keep repeating the process until the entire room is littered with wrapping paper and empty boxes but devoid of focused attention and appreciation. All we are doing is training them to not enjoy the thing in their hand as much as the next thing, which then becomes the thing in their hand (rinse and repeat). These effects can carry over into other parts of their lives and they may find it hard to stay interested in jobs, friends or family rather than searching for the next thing.

 We build this obstruction in ourselves with the amount of tv channels, music, websites, apps, clothing, devices, the advertisements for all of them and everything else that you can think of. I can only imagine that this obstacle will grow even higher as the choices for all of these things grow, as they surely will. Our brains are beyond astonishing and will surely adapt to this over time but we do still have some control here and now. We can start paying attention to the thing in our hand and learning everything that we can from it before even caring about the fact that there is a next thing. Apply this to all of the things listed above but especially those jobs, friends and family. Do this and not only will you waste less and learn more but I am betting that you are happier because of it. Give this gift to your child instead of the latest gadget or toy so that they might be able to have more appreciation for every thing, not just the next one. It isn't the stuff, the things or tv that's responsible. It should be the one that decides what to choose held accountable.

 We make our kids wear uniforms to school to stop bullying. Why would we punish everyone instead of just punishing the bully? For one, it doesn't stop the bullying and for two, you are punishing the whole to stop the few (not holding the right person accountable). I think that bullying is a normal occurrence in real life after school and that they better find ways of coping with it at a younger age while they have the safety net of teachers and loved ones around to guide them through it. This way they will have someone around that can help them to deal with each different set of circumstances.

 If you were able to make the bullying in school stop completely, and those students made it through it and out into the real world without ever encountering such an obstacle, it would be a much larger challenge once confronted. It's like trying to learn a new language, which is much easier when we are young and our brains are built for processing new information. It is a much more daunting task to relearn something that has been engrained over time. They would have to do this far from that caring support group and despite the ones that want to bully them, the ones that want their job and the ones that just don't care, instead of being helped.

 When a dog bites a person they put the dog down, even though it was the owner's responsibility to keep it contained and make sure that the dog wasn't a danger to others. I bet if we started putting owners down instead, you would see a lot more responsible dog owners and lot less dog bites.

 We blame the cigarette companies because we like their product too much instead of the person that decides to keep smoking and get cancer. We tax those cigarettes heavily to pay for things like football stadiums. Why not just tax the football fans or the people that want the stadium by making those football stadium related items more heavily taxed? Because that would be holding the right person accountable and that's just not what we do.

Smoking is a choice that we make for ourselves. Contrary to popular belief, it is not the ads that make you smoke, it is the fact that you like to smoke. I see ads all of the time for feminine hygiene products but manage to not go out and buy them. If you don't like that analogy, the same thing goes for beer advertisements. I buy cigarettes because my dumb ass likes to smoke. It isn't the cigarette companies fault that I like their product any more than it is McDonald's fault that the fat bastard likes their burgers. You don't run out and buy things that you don't like because of the ads, you buy the things from the ads that interest you. We are responsible for the decisions that we make, whether it is our weakness, our ignorance, lack of will power or just the sheer enjoyment of the thing, we alone should be held accountable because we, and no one else, are responsible for our own actions.

We are so against smoking because of the "danger" that it poses to life. This is about the most hypocritical train of thought seeing as how society has made the choice to allow murder, as long as it comes at an early enough age. They call it abortion but it is no less of a crime because of the name. I'm not saying that there may not be examples of it being an acceptable option. Such is the case of rape, the fetus not being compatible with life or because it threatens the life of the mother. But those are about the only times that I can view it as even close to a worthy option.

What is almost as appalling is that the woman has the right to choose! This wouldn't be as sickening if the man were not expected to take on 50% of the burden in the future but this is not the case. The man is expected to support the child to the tune of at least half. I totally agree with this and would view any man that wouldn't support his child as not a man at all. Each party had a hand in making the baby, therefore each party should have equal right to say what will happen with the baby along with an equal burden of support afterwards. How could anyone disagree with this simple fact without the thought being selfish and ignorant? Trick question, the answer is; they couldn't.

There aren't too many things in this world that can send a shudder down a man's spine like hearing the words, "the child is considered property and automatically owned by the mother". This is a real fucking thing!!! These are words that I guarantee will get a judge shot at some point. If I'd have lost my custody case, this would have already happened. I am a responsible, capable, loving father and am not the only one that has heard this deplorable sentence spoken to them as if it is not even their child. There is no law that will tell me that "my" child is not mine and that I don't have equal claim to it. They don't get to make that choice. They sure would've expected it to be "my" child when it came time to pay child support. I follow the law of right, not the law of the land and they got lucky that they made the right decision that day or they would have deservingly experienced the ravenous fury of a tenacious father's wrath. That wouldn't have been good for any of the parties involved (including myself) but would have been unavoidable. This system needs to change before a father is forced into making these same decisions (to protect his child) when the court fails to make the right decision (when, not if).

We are supposed to have equal rights, are we not? Then where are the man's rights at the time of conception and after? Where are the child's rights? At this point, in this country at least, the man and the child have no rights. The woman has the right to choose. The only rights the other people have are, the man has the right to pay and the child has the right to die. I'm no math major or constitutional lawyer but I'm almost positive that those rights aren't equal. If equality of rights and the choice of what to do with another person's body (which is what abortion is) is so integral to a woman's rights, then by simple deduction, they would have to accept anyone's choice to end anyone's life. So, if she chooses to end that life, all rights being equal, someone should be able to choose to end hers, correct? See where this idiotic logic leads?

Of course women should be treated equally. Only a thoughtless fucksack would think otherwise. We should all have the same rights, but that equality is exactly what decides that it is not "her" choice alone because the man and the child have rights as well that are equal, not lesser than hers. Man or woman, if you think that it is your choice then, congratulations, you are that thoughtless sack of fuck. Add to that, the fact that you don't believe in equal rights, and if that is the case then let's do away with equality in the home, workplace and voting booth and see how you feel then. You don't get to have your cake and kill it too.

One way to keep this from happening might be to institute a system of protection for the children such as: If a woman wants an abortion and the man wants to keep the baby, the woman should have to carry the baby to term and then give up custodial rights to the child and pay support until it's an adult. If the man wants the abortion but the woman wants to keep it, the man should sign over his rights to the child and pay support until it's an adult. If neither party wants the child, they should have to have it anyway and be held liable for any damages occurring to the child. If the child should have to be taken in to foster care because of neglect or harm, the parents should be held in a city-controlled work camp that produces goods that's profits go directly to the community and the foster care system that their child is in until the child is an adult. I can only imagine that this would lead to people trying to profit from the situation but measures would have to be in place to make it a heinously unrewarding and highly punishable endeavor.

There are obviously holes in this idea, and that is all that it is, an idea. I'm not saying it's a great one, but I think you get my drift. This is a problem that needs to be tackled by many minds greater than mine. It doesn't seem that this was the case previously, given the solution that resulted from it. Neither party should be able to sanction a murder just because they didn't want to wear a condom, forgot to pull out or got too drunk and made a poor decision. They should be held accountable, but instead we murder the child as if it were responsible for their parents' irresponsibility. We need to stop holding the future's youths responsible for our transgressions, mistakes and selfish decisions. Don't want a kid, don't have sex. If having sex is that important, then be prepared to take responsibility for your actions or keep it in your pants. Please don't go thinking that it is your job to populate the earth, because it is not the case at all. It only takes one trip to Wal-Mart to find out that not everybody should pro-create. Please study a mirror, take an I.Q. test, check your family's physical and mental history and find out from others what kind of a person you are before you decide you are one of the ones that should.

I don't care if this pisses you off. You have a right to your opinion, but that doesn't make your opinion right. These are not my opinions but are factualized by the fact that you are reading this book rather than having been aborted yourself. I'm pretty sure that you are happy that you weren't aborted and if not, you can still abort yourself. It is, after all, the type of abortion (suicide) that I am a fan and a proponent of.

Suicide is illegal. Soak that in for a second…… suicide is illegal but abortion isn't. A person that does not want to be alive is not allowed to end their own life but they are allowed to end the lives of countless others (abortions) with no legal ramifications even if it was just because they were drunk or ejaculated prematurely. The person that is not born yet does not even get the chance to decide whether it wants to live. If this makes sense to you, then you are the one that is calling your intelligence and compassion into question, not me. If what I'm saying does piss you off, then it may just be an immoral core, ignorance or lack of rational thought that cloud your mind enough to not see this blatantly obvious truth. This makes you exactly the special kind of dumbass that I enjoy pissing off.

In our government, the representatives are responsible for conveying the people's opinion. They are elected on what tend to be false promises, take money from special interest groups and regularly fail at their job but aren't held accountable. When they "are" it is never to the extent necessary and far less than a citizen would receive for the same offense. This isn't to say that every politician is bad. I think that a large portion of the people that get involved in politics do it for the right reasons and genuinely want to make a difference. I also think that when they get there they see how corrupt the system is and feel that their efforts would be futile at best so they just join them rather than fight what they believe to be a losing battle. There are also politicians that have been trying to fight that losing battle for decades without voting yes on stupid bills or even taking pay raises. Ron Paul is the only person that I can think of that fits all 3 of these. I'm sure there are thousands more that might even get 1 or 2 out of 3 that are just as effectively powerless without the aid of those that give in instead. The point is that good politicians are out there, they just don't stay that way for long and if they do they are few and farther than far between.

 In this recent election (2016), I heard one sentiment echoed over and over, "we need someone that's not a politician". I have a hard time finding the logic in this statement but I get the reasoning. I get it because it does seem like the current system is broken and all we see are politicians that are to blame. News flash….the people that know about politics are politicians. You need to have a politician do that job for that reason.

 This is no different than if you were having car trouble, you obviously need a mechanic. So, you take your car to a mechanic that tells you that your blinker fluid being low caused an issue that costs you 500 dollars. You pay the money and drive away just to find that the issue hasn't been taken care of at all. You then decide to take it to a different mechanic instead of back to the guy that just proved himself incapable. This mechanic says that the other guy was lying to you, there's no such thing as blinker fluid and that the real problem is with your compression vortex interface coupling (also not real). This costs you 1000 dollars and you drive away just to find that, not only do you still have the same problem, but now it's worse. You call the BBB and the police but there isn't anything anyone can do to help you. It starts to seem like all of these shiesty grease monkeys are just taking you for a ride and can get away with anything (just like politicians). So, what do you do now, go find someone that isn't a mechanic? A banker perhaps, maybe a fry cook? No genius, you just need to find a good mechanic instead of the poor excuses for them that you have used previously.

You've been serviced by shitty politicians, so hold them accountable and replace them with good politicians. In this case you have just traded in skunks for a weasel. Sure, they may have stunk but that's about it, other than maybe getting in your trash. This long thought relative, though, that you chose to replace the skunks, is a voracious hunter who will kill more than he can eat and is only out for himself. He is just a corrupt politician that used "business man" rather than politician as a title. He is definitely as corrupt and probably more so, but just lacks the knowledge and experience necessary to do the job, the character you want from a leader or the morals of the most reputable despot. I don't see a Mensa membership in your future as a reward for your choice.

You just stood outside of the first bad wig shop you could find and asked some random guy walking out to fix your country. How does this make sense? It doesn't matter, you won't even hold yourself accountable. I'm sure you'll find a way to blame it on someone else. If we would hold the right people accountable we wouldn't be in this mess. Because of this, like it or not, we are responsible and should hold ourselves accountable and do something to change this broken system.

Instead, we are still fooled (some of us) by what we are led to believe by the ones that stand to gain (people that want to control you). We make irrational judgements out of fear or anger without facts or logic to guide them and misplace responsibility too regularly. This is the case with the rise in the number of school shootings. There is an immediate reaction for gun control as if the object is the cause of the problem rather than the person controlling the object.

When and where I grew up and went to school there were many kids that drove to school with gun racks in the window of their truck. The racks were holding what they were intended for and named after, the doors were seldom locked and I never heard a shot or saw a gunman. People had buck knives and pocket knives on their person every day, I was one of them, and didn't feel the need to use them. Even when there were arguments or fights, you put your fists up and swung 'em around until one or both of you didn't want to do it anymore and that was the end of it. I was a part of getting and giving those ass-kickings in school and managed not to stab anyone or get stabbed. Our school wasn't the exception, but the rule, no news of anything of the sort from any of the surrounding schools either. This was only two decades ago, not in the 40's or 50's.

 I have a hard time, believing that those inanimate objects acquired the magical powers necessary to perform these acts on their own over the last 20 years. That being said, I have to look elsewhere for blame. We had arguments, disagreements, bullying and everything else (minus social media, but that's your own fault for giving it that power in your life). Believe me, when I went to school everybody knew what you had for dinner last night, if they wanted to and even when they didn't, kids talk (even back then). You decide what to put out there, and how much power to give what's coming back.

 I knew the justice system of our school better than most students by leaps, cracks, suspensions, expulsions and bounds. I was what one might consider unruly but I was really just bored out of my mind. I hated the entitled preppy fuckstains at my school that looked down on the kids that didn't have the coolest or cleanest clothes or cars. I didn't have parents around that gave a shit about me or what I was doing and sought refuge with the wrong crowd (that I thought cared about me). None of the circumstances were in my control but the way to deal with them was, and all of those choices that I made were mine. Still, being one of the more "unruly" kids within a hundred miles, and with weapons at my disposal I managed not to storm the school. As did all of the other kids within hundreds of miles, that got bullied, picked on, singled out or that were just plain sick of it.

At some point you have to stop trying to place the blame on someone else and hold the ones behind the object accountable. Many will say that it is because we took god out of the schools as if the lord would keep the violence from occurring. If this were the case, I would have to wonder why he has such a hard time keeping pedophilia out of the church or wars from being waged in his name? I realize that parenting comes into play along with prescribed meds, desensitization to violence and many other personal or societal factors. These are all problems that need to be addressed, but at the end of the day they are all choices that were made or that allowed things to continue. Those choices were made by the individual and by their parents.

The way that we use these things or objects is what should be in question and the we that misuses it should be held accountable. The gun is the same inanimate object that it ever was. It is the we behind that gun and the why behind that we that is to blame. It's the we that has changed, not the gun, and the we needs to quit passing the buck of blame and start realizing that fact before un-fucking this world becomes an even more seemingly insurmountable task.

FLAGS AND MUSIC

Flags are another way that we choose to separate ourselves. They fall into the "chosen for us" category as well because we don't have any control over where we are born. The individual, however, is the one that chooses to continue to back, glorify, pledge allegiance to or even kill for them. Just because you are born in a place does not make it better than another. It doesn't make the people that live in that place worse people than you. If it does, since you were born in a different place than them, then in their eyes doesn't that make their place better than yours and you worse people than them? If they pledge their allegiance to a different flag it does. This very sentiment has started far too many wars; This is mine, my stuff is better, I don't like your stuff or I want your stuff and I'm going to take it.

We are all too accepting of actions and behaviors from the leaders of our countries that we wouldn't even think of accepting from a child in school. We shouldn't allow a child to push other kids down and take their toys just because he's from the east side. Grow him up and give him a flag and the same actions, and this makes him a patriot. Unless of course he flies a different colored flag, then he's a terrorist. It is absolute idiocy. More correctly, I think, it is just basic human greed that none of us can completely overcome but that some are just more susceptible to than others. Even if it's just I want a new phone, a bigger yard or I don't want to die, it's greed.

Basically, greed is having all that you need and wanting more. This is what got us out of the cave, what made us start farming, building machines and even the cure for polio. Whether or not these are good things is up for debate and is one that I rather like to have. It is also what gave us war mongers, mass genocide and biological weapons. There again, greed is a tool that we didn't choose but that we all have and choose to use in very different ways.

We teach people at an extremely young, impressionable age to blindly pledge their allegiance regardless of whether their leaders are shitty human beings or that those leaders and their beliefs change every few years. To do so without thought of bought off elections, scandals and the choice between dumb and dumber. Regardless of wars for profit at the cost of our children! It's ok to do it because it's us and those extremist bastards on the other side of the planet must be stopped! Even at the expense of their own innocent civilians that we are "protecting"! I realize all of our ironic similarities, but those bastards is crazy! We on the other hand are patriots!

I was taught the same thing when I was a child. It was the early 80's and I thought for sure that we were going to die in a nuclear war. If it wasn't for the newspapers, radio, tv, movies or overheard adult's conversations promising that the threat is real, then maybe it wouldn't have been an issue. Be that as it may, my parents had the added benefit of being able to tell me that my 6th great Aunt was Betsy Ross. I don't think that they had any ulterior motives, but instead were just conveying and hoping to instill their own personal pride of the matter in me. It worked. This had me clicking my heels, covering my heart and regurgitating the pledge with the rest of the herd. My words came through a delighted, unalloyed smile and my heart swelled with pride because someone that I was related to sewed the first American flag. I had many relatives that were in the military and that made me feel proud as well because they "fought for our freedom". Every time I heard the National Anthem, no matter where I was, I stood up, along with every hair on the back of my neck. You would have had a hard time finding someone that felt more patriotic. But I had been propagandized!

Finding out that there isn't a shred of evidence that proves that Betsy sewed the first flag was upsetting. Not because of the fact that there is a man named Francis

Hopkinson that has a stronger claim but because they made up her story and keep telling it because it is exactly that, a better story (propagating the faith). That blow was followed by knowledge bombs of lies, deception and the outright theft of our country by the very people that are "elected" to protect it. This feeling of betrayal was exaggerated even more by a government and military industrial complex that was more worried about oil, drugs and flexing their nuclear muscles than they were about the innocent civilians of those we were at war with or the ones they were supposedly fighting for.

Now, I sit. My hair doesn't stand up either. Now I am almost sickened when I see a stadium or gymnasium full of followers covering their hearts and beaming with programmed, nationalistic pride (can you say Nazi). I say almost because I know that a lot of them just don't have a clue, and because I used to be just as clueless. I am thankful that my mind wasn't too weak to break those chauvinistic chains and I hope that the same truth finds its way into the minds of everyone that is still guzzling the Kool-Aid. I love the country that I'm from, but that shouldn't lessen my love for another. Again, I will let their actions be the judge of that (the actions of the people, not their leaders). I just don't see any reason that being born in one place makes another place or the people that live in it not as good. If this were true, then you should feel that you are better than everyone because they didn't come from the same sperm, egg or womb that you came from.

I respect the men and women that serve, and my choice not to stand doesn't diminish that respect in the least. It is my respect for those people that makes both the blatant disregard for their lives and the propaganda distributed by their employers so disgusting. There's not the tiniest sliver of doubt to be had when I don't respect you, I tend to make it abundantly clear and sitting isn't the tool that I'd use. Given the alternatives, believe me, I am being respectful by sitting.

Flags tell someone that this is yours. Pledging your allegiance to them means pledging them against someone else's. If someone is doing the same thing for the same reasons but just saluting a different colored piece of cloth, then what makes you right and them wrong? Don't worry, the ironic similarities continue, your answer is the same as theirs too.

People that fly the same flag can't even agree on what that flag represents. If you look at what the colors and symbols on the South Carolina flag actually mean (look it up), they don't seem very offensive and they didn't represent racist ideas. The flag flew over a state that allowed slavery, true, but many people in that state then and now did not agree with those practices and still believed in what the flag was "supposed to symbolize". If this is grounds for removing a flag then I would argue that the American flag should be removed. It was born by malicious, greedy, racist intentions and has performed countless acts of destruction including Holocaust. It even effectively allowed slavery to continue in South Carolina and the rest of the south after reconstruction in return for the presidency (compromise of 1877). I think that it is moronically ironic that one would fly the American flag while screaming for the removal of another on those grounds. This country declared, along with its independence, that all men are created equal, yet even then only land owning white males were allowed to vote. I guess you can have somebody else's cake and eat it too, you just have to be a worse person than them.

Flags can be false as well. The term false flag comes from the days when piracy was the tool of the trade (not that it's much different today other than the vessels and the garb). It was used by thieves and emperors alike, not that there's much of a difference there either. Either way, the attacking ship would fly the home country's flag of the ship that was being attacked. They used this form of deception to allow themselves closer access and the element of surprise so that the enemy wasn't prepared to fight or as easily able to retreat. These practices have not gone out of style and are still paraded about the catwalk of the main stream media instead of flown on the mast of a ship. Sure, the outfits have changed, but the idea of deceiving your victims into making your job easier has not.

If you are a staunch advocate of the official account of the events of 9/11, then you are as delusional as the most devout conspiracy theorist that "knows" exactly how it "really" happened. Unless you were one of the perpetrators, then you don't know exactly what happened. What we do know for sure, is that the official account is rife with answers that just lead to more questions that they refuse to answer. We do also know that the some of the people that were heavily invested in the Carlyle Group (a Washington merchant bank specializing in defense and aerospace buyouts that stood to make billions from a war) were George Bush Sr. and the Bin Laden family (coincidence? I think not). It has also been proven that the U.S. government has a well-documented history of planning to deceive and actually deceiving the American public in order to gain their support for war or to disrupt domestic political organizations (U.S.S. Maine, Gulf of Tonkin, Operation Northwoods, the false Nayirah testimony, PNAC, COINTELPRO). The government has a long love affair with lies and deception during wartime, which when used against an opponent that means to do us harm is understandable. But as with most liars, the lies don't stop there. If you readily, and often lie to achieve your objective, then I have a hard time believing that you are going to be truthful with me. The same goes for any individual as well, if you will lie to me, even about something small, like what kind of ice cream is your favorite, then I know for a fact that you will lie to me to save your ass.

These types of events are not exclusive to the U.S. They have been used throughout time by the Romans, British, Germans and the Chinese just to name a few (Nero's burning of Rome that he blamed on the Christians, the

Zinoviev letter, Mukden incident, Gleiwitz incident) and probably countless other times that we have no account of.

There are numerous documented occasions where the government has gone even further to gain knowledge and increase its control by waging war on the minds of innocent civilians. In these cases, they used a much more direct approach. In the early 50's the C.I.A. performed mind control experiments on human subjects with Project Bluebird and Artichoke that led to the program called MKUltra. During that time, they used drugs (especially LSD), sensory deprivation, hypnosis, radiation, electro-shock therapy and various forms of psychological torture to alter the brain and manipulate people's mental state. The program wasn't officially "shut down" (yeah, right) until 1973. These tests didn't just happen on army bases. They also happened in colleges, hospitals, prisons and even a bedroom of a random San Francisco home, as in Operation Midnight Climax. They did these things in search of knowledge because knowledge is power. Controlling the body is easy, but you need power to control the mind. If you don't think that control is the goal, then yours may already be controlled.

People that are in control want to stay in control and people that want to be in control will, generally, not let much stand in the way of that goal even if it means lying, cheating, stealing and killing to get what they want. It even happens every day at your job. The people that are willing to inform, lie and comply always seem to be the ones that get the promotion instead of the person that keeps their head down and just does their job better than anybody else. This is precisely why it is not uncommon to find nothing but heartless shitbags in upper management of almost any operation. They want someone at the top that is going to whistle the company tune and sing the yeah yeahs in the background not a virtuoso that's going to steal the show.

Music is a magical form of expression that can be found throughout the world. It can be used to lift your spirits, make you sad, keep your mind off of a mundane task, for meditation and even to control the world. Music has been used for centuries by humans to call each other together for battle. It has been used with horns made from the horns of animals which gave them their name, with bagpipes in misty island hills, to signify an army charge with a bugle or even to elicit a programmed response. As when hearing an anthem that may make you feel that it's your patriotic duty to invade another country. At one-point Britain outlawed the use of bagpipes in Scotland because of their martial importance and in the 18th century enlisting in the army was described as "following the drum". It still permeates this and almost every other facet of our lives.

Blood flows like a cascade of arpeggios when it is used as the soundtrack in the theater of war. This has been the case for centuries and continues to this day. Whether it be Isis' use of nasheeds, Japanese gunka or Germany's Reichsmusikkammer, it knows no nation's boundaries and recruits intently. The findings of Annett Schirmer, reported at the Society for Neuroscience meeting in New Orleans, show that music can do more than just control emotion and movement. It can actually control the brain circuitry of sensory perception. Unfortunately, it doesn't surprise me anymore at all to think that these greedy entities have used one of the most beautiful things that we do to cause such destruction. Music is an extremely powerful tool, to say the very least, but again people use it in many different ways. Even when the intention is the same, such as changing thought or the world, Hitler and John Lennon chose to use music in an entirely different way.

Music that we decide that we like, or that we decide that we despise, also separates us from each other. If you are at a hip-hop concert, then you are not at the death metal concert across the street, therefore not connecting with any of those individuals by choice. Even if you wanted to go to both shows, because you like both of the bands, you still chose the hip hop concert. Sometimes you make the choice because your disdain for a type of music comes from its lyrical content and the fact that it berates your beliefs, ideals or even your race. You may even choose not to associate with people that could like or believe such a thing. Sometimes it is because of sounds or instruments that you find annoying or even physically unsettling. Still, others may not like something because of the lack of truth from the artist or because it was churned out by commercializing music executives. In any case, we are making the choice to like or not like the music or the people associated with it. It could also easily be argued that we like what we like because we are the individual person that we are and that we had no choice in the matter of how a sound affects our brain.

 People are raised around certain types of beliefs and music and instead gravitate to types that are polar opposites all of the time. Sure, sometimes it's to buck the system, but it can just as easily be because that new music affects that person's brain in an exciting way that they hadn't previously been exposed to. Either way, you choose to continue listening, feeling and maybe even alienating, so it's still a choice (or is it?).

 Music has been an instrumental driving force in my life that has helped to shape who I am in more ways than most. I have a much larger view of ideas, feelings, other cultures and even vocabulary because of it in particular. That's not even counting the life changing relationships that I've made or the information that I've collected from them. Some of the most beautiful experiences I have ever had were intrinsically music related. I still find myself asking if others feel the same way about the concert that they are at right now. I wonder that if I had traveled a different path, would that be the music that excites my senses or is the message, people and vibe of the concert that I am at the only thing that could ever have brought on those types of feelings? Either way, I chose not to be at that other concert, to take myself away from those individuals and my life will be different because of it. At

39

the same time, I make connections that will forever change me and my future. Whether this is a good thing or not can't possibly be known until the end, and I just have to use my best judgement and a healthy dose of compassion and hope that my intentions are pure. In any case, I still make the choice and should be the one held accountable.

I truly believe that music is one of the most relevant things that we do and along with the other arts, is what makes us human. This is not to say that other species don't make music or art but it would be hard to argue that any do it to the degree or with the complexity and passion that we do. I think music is the culmination of all of the arts. It takes parts from the lyrical flow of poetry and elicits visions more beautiful than any painting with its notes, chords, feel and moods. It is acting, storytelling and the reason that we dance. I have a great deal of respect for all of the arts and think that they are all necessary for your mind, but I feel that music has the best bits of all of them and a more in-depth way of affecting people in general.

I went to a concert in Minnesota in my 20's with 1000 t-shirts and a dream. I designed them and went to the show solely in hopes of making money. I was greeted at the gate with the words; welcome home. I thought, "I must look like a guy that frequents this place" as I left in search of a place to pitch my tent. The second and third time I heard it I thought, "I must look a lot like this guy", that lucky bastard. The next time I figured it out, this was just their hippy-dippy way of telling me that I'm at home now, how lame.

This was, what most would call, a "hippy" music festival. My t-shirts fit the bill but I sure didn't. I was surrounded by patchwork, frisbees, hacky sacks, hand drums and an absolutely horrible aroma (patchouli). I on the other hand was wearing high tops, cutoff jeans and a Slayer shirt. I had my booth set up really nice, even had some tunes jamming (Suicidal Tendencies) and couldn't figure out for the life of me why more people weren't stopping by. Lol. I was not a happy camper and couldn't wait to leave Saturday night to get home in time to watch the game.

That weekend I was introduced to people, music and thoughts that would change my life forever. I know what you're thinking; hippy show plus life changing music and thoughts equals drugs. Wrong. As much as I was hoping to score something for the head, I didn't and I wasn't happy about that either, at first. Our campsite neighbors, my vending neighbors (rabbit in particular) and all of the other bliss junkies that I met that weekend changed my perspective on what my perception of a "hippy music festival" was. Until that point, I hadn't met too many people that listened to music the way I did, that breathed it. Listening to every note and tearing the lyrics apart to find the meaning, excited by every time change and clinging to every crescendo. It was music nirvana, a Shangri-La of sorts. The music that was there was all so full of life, fun and spectacular musicianship. I didn't leave

Saturday night. As a matter of fact, my partner had a hard time dragging me out of there at all.

I did leave the park late Sunday morning though, albeit in tears, after multiple hugs and to a glorious harmony of I love yous. I did so muttering one word; Wookiefoot! All the way back to Oklahoma, Wookiefoot. This band and the community that surrounds them are some of the most special people that I have encountered. I encourage you, no matter what kind of music you prefer, to give them more than just a listen. Study would be a much better word. Their message is as thought provoking and positive as you could ever hope to find and their musical styles run the gamut.

After I left, I searched out other festivals and found a lot of likeminded people but after the festivals I still went home. It didn't take long for me to realize that home wasn't home any more. The show, the road, the journey was home now. I lived on the road for a little more than 3 years with my roommate and 3 dogs in an R.V. until I decided, with the help of a few friends, that we should throw our own show. I went back to the venue that was the site for my first concert experience. I could not have been more excited. We had all of the bands contracted, staff organized, porta-johns secured and utilities taken care of. It was going to be epic……. until we got ripped off to the tune of about 20k. One of our partners bought the insurance under a business name that was enough like ours that the venue owner didn't catch it, thereby essentially hijacking our festival. I was heartbroken, broke and stuck in Ohio, could this be any worse? I stayed at a buddy of mine's house, feeling sorry for myself, for what was supposed to be a few days, maybe a week. That is when the most magical part of my life began to take form.

 If the show would have gone off without a hitch, I wouldn't have stayed in Ohio. I wouldn't have hooked up with a chic from high school and she wouldn't have gotten pregnant, despite our best efforts towards that not being the case. Right at the moment that I didn't know what I was going to do, when I thought that it couldn't get much worse, I got the best news that I had ever gotten or will ever get. I was going to be a dad! So, like Jerry said, "sometimes you get shown the light in the strangest of places if you look at it right". And it doesn't get much stranger than living in Zanesville. Music made more than my day, it made my life! And to this day, welcome home are two of my favorite words to hear (and as far away from lame as can be). I still can't stand patchouli!

FOOTBALL AND RESPECT

 Football, no matter how you spell it, is big business. It is one of the biggest cash cows that the entertainment industry has in the slaughterhouse. It brings in billions of dollars a year and it's no wonder that it does when you consider what it costs just to go to a game. First you have to make sure that you have the 200 dollar jersey and at least that much in accessories (towel, hat, face paint, helmet, batteries, spike covered shoulder pads, etc.) before you put the team flags on the car. Then you have to pay to park, shell out 100 dollars or more for a ticket and whatever you spent on your tailgate spread. Even if you forego the pregame festivities and just park and go straight into the stadium there are still plenty of 4 dollar waters, 8 dollar hotdogs and 12 dollar beers to be had. There is also plenty of other overpriced swag like programs, t-shirts, hats and other memorabilia to test your wallet's limits. Don't worry, going to the game isn't the only way to feed the machine. Sponsorship works too, providing you are already filthy stinking rich and can afford the exorbitant fee.

 Together they make up only half of the NFL's revenue. The other half is funded by the average Joe watching the game on television from his couch or at the bar. Paying for things like cable and the Sunday ticket are a couple of the biggest factors helping to make up that 7-billion-dollar half of their total revenue. If everyone would get on the same page and stop watching the NFL in any form until those prices came down to a reasonable level it would take one game (maybe) for the owners to drop the prices. If they are then making millions instead of billions, then they could pay the players 10's to 100's of thousands instead of millions and we would be on a somewhat more realistic scale. It wouldn't hurt the talent pool any and the same people will still play the games. It's not like these guys are going to go use their "degrees" to make more money doing something else instead.

 I am not against anyone capitalizing on their talents and I believe that the players have every right to want a piece of the pie, of which they are the filling. The filling being the main attraction, is after all, why you buy the pie. The crust that holds that pie is the coaching staff, trainers, scouts and every other employee that helps to prepare the team. The crust is almost, if not, as important, but not usually why you buy the pie. In this metaphor, the owner is the pie pan and when is the last time that you bought a pie because of the pan? So, I get why the players want, and in my opinion, deserve a large percentage of those profits. Those profits are there because we decide to spend our hard-earned money and our time watching a game. Too often it is the case that both could have been better spent elsewhere (family, community, teachers). This is just one instance of a growing social problem of caring too much about our entertainment, or at least what entertains us and how much we let it. We do the same thing with shopping, tv, movies, music and more but we'll get to that later.

Think about it; do you really want some guy that throws a ball for your entertainment to make more than the people that teach your children how to be mechanics, engineers and doctors? If so, it would be hilariously ironic to see your car break down on a poorly engineered bridge that then caused your life-threatening injury that the doctor was too stupid to be able to save you from. Maybe you'll get lucky and the game will come on just as you flatline. I would consider it a deserved fate.

This isn't to say that no good at all comes from sport. I love competition. I think sports are a spectacular way to stay in shape both physically and mentally. Many long-lasting relationships and ideals are created through it, not to mention the charities that are formed and the donations that are given by players, owners and communities alike. I just think that when anything gets too big and profitable you have a problem, and the problem is that all-inclusive, basic human staple, greed. Money starts to become more important than morals.

Caring more about our entertainment than our education is one of the worst mistakes that I believe that we can make and every generation is going to be worse off because of it. There are families that are torn apart because of seemingly petty rivalries over football and futbol alike. In places like Buenos Aires, up to 70 people at one time have died because of fires, stampedes and fan/police violence not to mention multiple beatings and stabbings. In east London the police have a very strong presence on the field but there is little they can do when violence breaks out between 10's of thousands of fans, other than do what little they can to try to protect the players. These incidents, whether they be because of the rivalry between the rich and poor (Buenos Aires) or between dock workers from a different dock (London) they are really just between people that hate each other for no other reason than that they are on the other side of the "game". Not even in the game, just watching. This isn't something that they are truly angry about. It is a scam.

I have been a victim of this scam. I grew up watching football and just like any other Buckeye fan, was taught that the team up north (meatchicken) was an option only for the less educated, morally suspect, and the people that drink more than their I.Q. before lunch. In the N.F.L. I rooted for the Steelers because, where I lived, that was who was on tv every Sunday. I grew up hating the Browns because of rivalry and the cowboys because they had the nerve to call themselves America's team. I became so engulfed by football that my identity was largely tied to it. I wore the gear, watched every game, knew all of the stats, had all of the swag, reveled in the wins, fought about the losses and even named my daughter after a stadium.

So much of my life was taken from me by making the choice to let a game played by millionaires for the benefit of billionaires be of so much importance to me. Again, it is not football's fault, but my own lack of diligence and attention to my wellbeing. Having come to this realization, I have a much healthier relationship with football now, although only with college at this time. I don't buy the gear, I watch some of the games and the wins and losses don't matter at all like they used to. My daughter's name hasn't changed and is almost as beautiful as she is regardless of the way that it came about. It is a reminder to me that things are only as powerful as we allow them to be and that beauty can be found in just about anything.

As for the N.F.L., you couldn't have met a bigger fan than myself. Even when I moved to Oklahoma, we turned our 4 to 5 person watch party at the bar into 300 strong meeting every Sunday to swing towels, point foam fingers and drink touchdown shots while rooting on our beloved Steelers. My daughter is named after the home stadium that they played in when they won their first super bowl. Hell, I even named their mascot "Steely McBeam". Little did the organization know that this was also a nod to the Grateful Dead's logo, a steal your face, commonly referred to as a steely.

 That all ended the day that they hired Michael Vick. I had fooled myself into believing that I rooted for the team because of their front office and recruiting prowess along with the code of morals and ethics that I saw lacking in other organizations. I was under the impression that they were a character first organization, not to be confused with the lesser teams that would pay you the big bucks as long as you won games, regardless of character. I was wrong.

 Moments after the decision to quit watching the team, I realized that the league was really to blame for even allowing him to put in an application. I was done giving my hard-earned money and even more valuable time to a league that could care less about me than whether a rapist, wife beater or murderer gets a second chance. I was done watching people assault each other after the play and not be prosecuted by the law the same way that any other citizen would if he punched a guy in the face at a pickup game in the park. I was done watching organizations move their teams while the fans that had supported them for so long could do nothing to stop them. All for the almighty dollar.

 Believe it or not, this was the most painful when that taint tasting sleazebag moved the Browns to Baltimore. You can't find more loyal fans than the Browns have. I would say that they are fans of the team and not of football or they would've stopped watching a long time ago, but that is beside the point. The loyalty of that fanbase is as undeniable as their willingness to show up every Sunday without fail, win (ha-ha) or lose. Despite that, they were powerless to stop the move and I saw, at that point, that if a fanbase that strong can have the turf yanked out from under their feet, then it could happen to anybody. I was done caring so much about something that would never care about me. In doing so, I questioned a lot of the other decisions I was making and re-evaluated what was of importance to me.

 The recent uproar surrounding the players kneeling for the national anthem and the misinformed, idiotic bigots that are not watching because of it, was almost enough to make me start watching again just out of spite. Partly because of the people dumb enough to base their disapproval solely on this. For this but not for the Ray Rice, Ray Lewis and Mike Vick type incidents becoming all too prevalent, as if they have such high moral standards? But mostly because of the fact that kneeling (a common sign of respect) is not mentioned as disrespectful in the flag code, or anywhere else that I can think of for that matter. What is mentioned, however, is the fact that the flag should not be worn on clothing. Yet people salute with honor from the bleachers wearing their flag t-shirt, bandana or pin, as men in uniform, wearing it stitched to said uniforms, watch the flag carried out horizontally not being allowed to fall freely. The latter act is also considered disrespectful by the flag code. Can you smell what the hypocrisy is cooking?

I can't stand flags! I don't see how they can ever be used for good. Regardless of intention, they only compartmentalize us. As much as we think that they unite us, all they really do is create a divide. They have been used since their inception to do that very thing. They are used to breed a sense of pride in one's homeland above the interests of all others. In doing so, they have helped to rape, pillage, kill and enslave lands, ideas, knowledge and countless human lives. These are the lives of the expendable people of the nations at war, not the sons and daughters of the people that start and fund them. The ideals of the people behind these swatches of fabric, on the other hand, matter infinitely more than any pile of thread ever could. If we could realize this, we could start breaking down the barriers that these bad forms of separation have built.

Most of the problem comes from people misunderstanding, not knowing and blindly pledging allegiance to something. Even when spelled out in black and white, some people will say, "of course it says that, but that's different in this case" or " yeah, but I'm wearing it out of respect, so that doesn't count". People will tell themselves just about anything to rationalize their own beliefs even when it goes against the very words that their belief is based upon.

Such is the case with the kneeling fiasco. If you have a problem with people kneeling to protest during the anthem or at any other time for that matter, I respect your right to your opinion. Just know that it differs from the definition of "freedom" that the flag that you so readily defend is supposed to signify. Any soldier worth a shit would be saddened by your misunderstanding of freedom and if not, they should not be allowed to be a soldier because they are not fighting for freedom, but instead for their own confused definition of it. Aren't the freedom of expression and right to peaceful protest supposed to be protected by your flag? Is not dissent the greatest example of patriotism? Then why would you vilify a person that is obviously a supporter, believer and practitioner of these same ideals? This, to me, proves that for the most part people make excuses, not to back the patriotic, ethnic or religious rhetoric of their flag as much as to back their own personal feelings, vendettas and agendas. I'm sorry (about your luck), but if you believe in and want freedom, this is exactly what it looks like. If you don't like the way that it looks, you just may not want freedom as badly as you think. Or maybe it is your definition that is confused.

 I don't care what kind of uniform you wear (civil or government) I do not blindly support you. If your actions prove you unworthy of thanks, trust or respect then you will get none from me regardless of your position or your self-perceived importance. This is only the case because it is how I treat every human being and your cover doesn't change the pages in between. Those pages (who you truly are inside) and your actions should decide how others treat you, not your apparel. I give every person that I meet my respect and let them and their actions decide how much of it they leave with.

Since I have fallen in love with photography, I have found countless ways that it has helped me to appreciate things. From seeing the things too small to see otherwise to understanding relationships between light and texture, but also the need to seek them out. I pay more attention to the weather, temperature, landscape and wildlife. I am enamored with the celestial bodies, old things as well as new and even moods, whether they come from the light, the color or the people that I photograph. It has given me a new-found respect for so many things and a way to capture some of the beauty that I see in this world without having to disturb it. It has allowed me to freeze time and remember that scene or my child's face as it will never be seen again. It has also taught me to do this when I don't have a camera in my hands. I look at everything differently and feel like I am a better me because of it.

One of the ways that I equate my camera to life is that when you use a camera to take a picture of an object you can change the look of that object dramatically by your position, as I spoke of before, but also with the lens that you choose to view it through. Using a wide-angle lens gives you a much different perspective than say a macro lens would. One is going to give you context and surroundings while the other will let you get so close that you could lose yourself in a raindrop. The same is the case for a telephoto lens and a fisheye lens. The telephoto is going to let you compress things and keep your distance while the fisheye gives you a distorted image that I think is great but that others don't like at all. There are many other types of lenses used to gain other perspectives but you get the idea.

Life is a lot like that and I have found that, just like in photography, if I change my mind's lens, it allows me to see thoughts and people differently. If I put the wrong lens on, I can get a very distorted picture of their thoughts and of them. In my mental studio, I am still learning to use all of the lenses at my disposal in the right way and I am getting better with it the more that I practice. For my mind, just like for my camera, I don't own every lens that I wish I had. There are some out there that I don't even know there is a need for. I am educating myself daily to find those lenses and am working diligently to acquire the ones that I know I need but don't yet have. I don't think that I'll ever master people, thought or photography but I am going to keep learning, growing and respecting them by trying to use the lens that will show me each individual's true light and respect the way that it was meant to be seen.

One of the things that can't be overlooked, no matter which lens you use, is that people are not the same. We come in many shapes and sizes and with just as many different beliefs and practices. That being said, there are still conclusions that you can draw about the whole once enough data is compiled.

People are too quick to pull the pc card these days and sometimes it feels as if that is all that is in their deck. I hear it more from women than I do from men but I believe that is due mainly to men controlling the majority of the power in society. This is changing more every day that we get farther from the caves where physical strength was more of a pre-requisite.

None of this is meant to take anything away from how special the female of our species is. Their rights should be equal because they are our equals. Being equals doesn't mean that we are the same, it means we deserve the same respect. We are obviously different, and in so many ways, but different doesn't mean better or worse. Our differences complement each other, as I believe they are meant to, and they are why we are such a proficient species. This is precisely the reason that I find it funny when people lash out when these differences are brought up as if that affects our equality.

Men are bigger and stronger than women as a whole. This is not a politically incorrect statement, this is a fact. That doesn't mean that there aren't women that are stronger than some men because there definitely are. These are the exceptions to the rule but it doesn't change the fact that this is generally the case. Women are more thoughtful and compassionate than men as a whole. This is a fact as well, even though there are many men that are more compassionate and thoughtful than some women. These exceptions don't change the facts but, in my eyes, only solidify the argument for our equality. We may not be equal in the amount of weight we can lift or how much we care, but that doesn't mean that the same sex wins every one of those battles or that we don't deserve the same respect regardless. Anyone who would argue this is a backwards gnikniht waste of flesh whose antiquated views will leave them at the back of the pack where they belong. "They" are the ones undeserving of that respect. Just remember to run your race, help when you can and don't look back, some things aren't worth saving.

RELIGION AND IDEAS

Religion is one of the biggest ways that we separate ourselves. It has caused as much death as old age and destroyed vast amounts of knowledge and information along the way. Much of the "belief" in a religion is chosen for you by your surroundings and even more so by your parents. The continued belief, however, is chosen by the individual. Sometimes because they aren't the type of person capable of breaking away from the societal standard or facing the fact that their parents could be wrong. Sometimes it is the fear of the repercussions of their faith (hell, no Valhalla, no 72 virgins. etc.) or the actual belief that they are right and that the thousands of other beliefs are wrong and that they're willing to bet their life on it. This is the beginning of the problem with religion; I'm right, everything else is wrong. The problem is that the other religions believe the same thing. This creates the reasoning, in the minds of rulers and followers alike, for wars, genocides, ethnic cleansings, terrorist acts and crusades. All well and good, I guess, if you're on the winning side but what are you winning when you dishonor your so-called beliefs in the process. Does it say thou shall not kill unless you are killing in my name? If so, I read a different version.

The fact is, that for the most part, religions are the same in the principle of; you do good, you get good. I actually think that most of them are describing the same story using other words and some geographic differences, but still the same story. That's why I think god is cheese. In some parts of the world it is fromage, in others it's queso but where I'm from, it's cheese. There are many types of it, different ways to make it, even different views of what each type should taste like but at the end of the day, it's all cheese. I think God, Allah, Buddha and the like are all just different ways of saying the same thing, they just don't taste as good on pizza:) My feeling is that religion probably got started out with good intentions. Maybe it was to calm yourself and not fear everything so much or a story to do the same for a child, but in the wrong hands, as with anything, it has become one of the deadliest weapons we have ever seen.

I have a saying, "religion is a manmade prison for your mind, for which spirituality is the key". I don't conform to a conventional religious belief but I try to respect and be good to everything I encounter from rocks to trees, from bugs to humans and future generations of all. I don't need to be told not to lie, cheat, steal or kill, I know that they're bad and I also know that there are times that I may have to do those things to stay alive or to protect my family, and that's not bad. The problem is that there are inevitably agendas, and the reasons for doing those very things get explained away by differently perceived scriptures and before you know it you're at war looking for weapons of mass destruction or getting rid of the infidels.

I wrote a poem when I was about 13 or 14 years old and it is still a belief I subscribe to today.

Man is a curious creature, too much is never enough.
We spare loved ones our time, for a piece of a dime,
as long as there's time to buy some more stuff.
We make up stories of gods and of prophets,
and accept them most with no proof.
Here's a passage from my little bible,
when you're dead then you'll know the truth.
Because up until then it's only just guessing,
the arguments only just noing and yessing.
All the time burdened by that weight you feel pressing,
the anchor of fear to say I don't know.

I shed the weight of that anchor long ago and embraced those three beautiful words. Today, I don't know is my belief. It was the same before I realized this, I just hadn't accepted it. I think that it is just about everybody else's belief too, whether they want to admit it or not. It is the only thing that there is proof of. Everything else is someone else's perception of what they've heard, read or their desire to falsify said knowledge for personal gain. The "believers" don't even know. They have faith, but faith just means "I don't know, but I'm betting all of my chips on this". So, even their belief's origin is rooted in, "I don't know". I don't know how the world was started and neither does anyone else, no matter what they say, think or believe.

We don't know about more than 90% of what's below the surface of the ocean and I'm supposed to believe that someone has creation nailed down? No one knows, because they weren't there and didn't see it. The same applies in a court of law and anything else is hearsay. For those that believe that they have been given the knowledge by a higher power, I would argue that; to even think of trying to say the name of something that created everything would be too much for your measly little brain to handle. I think that it's a very human thing that we think that it would have a name or that we would have similar features. It's funny that we always give the entities those human qualities, but we as humans only think like humans think. This doesn't mean that trees don't think. They just think like trees think and you don't know how to do that because you think like a human.

The largest living organism known to man is a humongous fungus that grows in the Blue Mountains of Oregon. In 1998 it covered an estimated area of 3.7 miles, beating the 1992 record of 2.4 miles consisting of the same type of fungus (honey fungus- Armillaria genus). The mushroom is just the fruiting body of a much larger organism called Mycelium which is basically (but not technically) a root system that searches out nutrients and new hosts. An organism refers to any individual living thing that can react to stimuli, reproduce, grow and maintain homeostasis and can also be defined by; being made up of genetically identical cells that can communicate, and that have a common purpose. By the latter definition, I would say that humans barely qualify.

Civilization as we know it is about 6000 years old, the modern form of humans an estimated 200,000 years and our ancestors about 6 million. Fungi on the other hand have been around for over 400 million years and many argue that the number is closer to 1700 million. These life forms have been communicating, co-existing and becoming one of the most prolific species of anything ever for hundreds of millions of years before we were ever even a twinkle in evolutions eye. Who's to say that we are smarter because we have thumbs, build bridges, have cars and air conditioning? Are fungi smarter for not needing those things? Are they living a more fulfilling life? I don't know, and I'm not afraid to say it. It is a liberating statement that opens the door to understanding. You'll never understand if you aren't willing to listen because you already know. Although, I do have a pretty good idea that if a child regularly asked his imaginary friend, Sam, for advice, gave him money and thought that he got to go to his house for eternity after he died that we would heavily medicate him, probably exorcise him and then promptly lock him up.

Anything past I don't know is just my best guess, that's all anybody's belief is, a best guess at best. Most of the time it is just what they were told or which one sounds the best.

 Don't think that I'm excluding science. It is a belief system as well, but more factually based and built upon being able to predict and reproduce results. For the most part it does a pretty good job of "answering" a lot of our questions and making our lives more comfortable. 2+2=4 is great and all, but when you get down to the quantum level our math ceases to make any sense. The same thing happens when you start talking about dark matter or black holes. It's called the big bang theory for a reason, it's just a theory. Yes, they provide very strong evidence for these theories but that is not proof. Theories are just your best guesses that are constantly fluctuating due to changes and new information. The biggest difference is that "most" scientists want to know the actual truth, not just prove their belief. Their beliefs are generally based on fact rather than the facts being based on their beliefs. Although, scientists are humans too, so you can bet that the latter does happen as well. We spend our lives believing these things as truth or searching for it. The truth is only what we know it to be until we get new information that shows us how wrong we are, thereby giving us a new truth. The truth is a lie. So far, in my opinion, science is just doing the best job telling it.

 I wonder incessantly about how we got here and I am still curious of whether there is a purpose. I have pondered reincarnation, multiverses and aliens as much as I've considered the matrix, the braneworld of M theory or just being worm food as options. I have even thought about whether our world is just a clump of dirt under a giant's fingernail. I find all of these to be just as plausible as there being one creator. I don't think that any of the organized religions have a clue either. They and their believers have just chosen their horse in the race. I haven't found a horse worth betting my life on yet, and I am beginning to think that the race is just a scam. Of course I have questioned whether there is a god (creator), and I continue to do so. I have a much harder time giving any validity to the use of compassionate as it's adjective.

 I absolutely appreciate and am awestruck daily by the beauty that I see in this world's land and seascapes, inhabitants and surrounding wonders (moons, planets, stars). I even realize the strength and resolve that can be gained from adversity. But it's things like hurricanes, tsunamis, earthquakes, Multiple sclerosis, downs syndrome, trisomy 13, or any other disease or natural disaster that make it so fantastically difficult to understand the use of the word compassionate when referring to it (god, creator).

 Random accidents or acts of violence that kill infants, or any other innocent people for that matter, also make it hard for me to see the "creator" in that light. I've heard the prodigiously poor excuse for an argument of, "you can't know god's will" or "the lord works in mysterious ways" too many times to count. It seems to me to be an erroneously convenient way to end your search. I would be upset if a movie that I had wasted my time watching ended that way. Mainly because the writers actually believed me to be dimwitted enough to buy that as an ending. You can't end it with, "your kids are dead, I knew it was going to happen and I created the thing that did it, oh, and I love you" and expect me to clap and cheer for your compassion. How could you settle for that as the answer to your biggest questions?

We were so upset with taxation without representation that a bunch of farmers went to war with a military super power but you don't expect any answer (representation) to, "why do innocent people die" from your "compassionate" creator? I've heard the, " that is the devil's work" argument for all of the bad that happens in the world and even the "free will" retort. My argument to that would be that if god is so omnipotent and knows everything, then he knew what the devil was going to do (when he created him) as well as what you were going to do with your free will. Therefore, it created that evil and knew what you would do with it or what it would do to you and intended them to be the case or would've done otherwise. So, he caused that shit to go down, heard your prayers and didn't give a fuck. This is compassion? If this is not the case, then omnipotence is not the case either which starts to bring a number of god's other powers into question.

If there is some thing that created everything, I can't imagine that we are much more than a science experiment to it, much like the dinosaur experiment from last year. At best, I would liken any "creator" theory to a kid today being given an ant farm instead of the iPad that he wanted. He might look at it from time to time. Sometimes he leaves it by the heater vent (drought, global warming), other times by the cold window (ice ages). Sometimes he shakes it just for fun (earthquakes) or pours water in it (floods, tsunamis), maybe even a fire cracker or two (volcanoes, cataclysms). But when he puts it down I doubt it enters his mind for days, maybe months or even eons as he goes about his life in a world that is far bigger than our little ant farm. I don't think that he'd be thinking about us while he was in class or on the way home from school, looking at his phone or talking to his friends. Let alone telepathically communicating with us to hear our prayers to help us win ball games, lotteries or, god forbid (ha-ha), to kill people.

 You can fit around 1 million earths inside of our nearest star (the sun). There are approximately 400 billion stars in our galaxy and about 100 billion galaxies in our universe and that is only as far as our telescopes let us see, for now. String theory suggests that there may be 10 to the 500th power universes and others theorize that pocket universes could be infinite. First, it makes it hard to believe (more like mathematically impossible) that we are the only ant farm sitting on one of the many shelves that that many universes would contain. Second, I doubt that the kid (god) makes it to our ant farm much, if at all, with everything else to be seen or tended to.

All of this being said, I can't and won't say that there is not a creator because I am not sure. I am unsure of pocket universes, reincarnation, aliens and the matrix as well to different degrees. I've said it before and am not in the least bit afraid to say it again; I don't know! And neither do you so quit giving people shit like you do know and just get along or get out of the way. Oh yeah, and quit driving slow in the left lane!!! If everybody did this we wouldn't have half of the wars that we do and probably even less than that. We might even learn something along the way.

There are as many Ideas of how we came to be or how we are supposed to be as there have been people. Some of them have caught on, others have failed miserably, while others still have gone unannounced. Christianity, Catholicism, Islam, Marxism, fascism, democracy, pacifism or almost any other set of beliefs have good parts that can be extrapolated from the doctrine itself. It is my belief, however, that none of them have it right mainly due to the fact that they believe in strict adherence to that set of rules or beliefs. I don't think that humans, or much else for that matter, work that way.

I think that you are doing yourself a disservice to not admit that you see evolution in our history. It can be seen in our hygiene, foods, language, technology, minds and bodies. To argue this is absolutely ludicrous. I'm not saying that we came from chimps but we sure don't live in caves anymore. You can plainly see, in any part of our world, that if something cannot adapt, it dies. The same thing has to hold true with these belief systems.

Bruce Lee had the same idea with the way he thought about martial arts. His fighting style mimicked his philosophy and I encourage you to look into that further on your own. Jeet Kune Do is a hybrid martial arts philosophy that he started in 1969 that takes useful parts from Wing Chun, boxing, fencing, Kali and kickboxing, among others, and incorporates them into kung Fu.

The UFC has seen the evolution of this. Long gone are the days of kickboxer vs. wrestler, judo vs. karate or ju-jitsu vs. sumo. It is called mixed martial arts now for a reason and if you go into the octagon today knowing only one discipline then you can expect to be tapping or napping before you get a chance to blink. Maybe we should start a mixed political arts league so that any antiquated singular form of logic can't compete.

I think that the only way we are ever going to be able to contend with a constantly changing opponent is to constantly change as well. We will need to be able to change our tactics in order to adapt to any situation. Bruce said, "Empty your mind, be formless, shapeless like water. If you put water into a cup, it becomes the cup. You put water into a bottle, it becomes the bottle. You put it in a teapot and it becomes the teapot. Now water can flow, or it can crash. Be water, my friend". I think, that in this way maybe all of these systems need watered down. We should fill our thoughts, beliefs and political systems with water. Not that toxic shit that they call water these days (keeping up with the Jones', crooked politicians, pedophilic priests, greedy leaders), but fresh, clean, pure water that hasn't been bought and sold, packaged or labeled. We can let some of it gently flow around the parts worth keeping and we should crash defiantly against the rest. Then "we" will be those belief systems. So, be water, my friends, and pour yourself into everything you do.

In the aftermath of the recent circus freak show, I mean U.S. election, I have heard many times that you shouldn't pass judgement on people because of their thoughts or political beliefs but I beg to differ. The way someone thinks and believes (along with their actions) is who they are and is exactly why you should choose to, or not to be around them. If we can't judge a person by their looks either, then what are we left with? If someone wrote in Charles Manson's name because they truly thought he was the man for the job, would you let them watch your kids tonight? If so, you're a dumbass.

We should take those things into account when we are deciding who to be around or who to let be around our kids. We do it every day in good ways, you take your kids to the nicest daycare that you can afford, not to the psych ward to have the guy that just stabbed 13 kittens watch them, good idea.

If, in this election, you were ok with those being the only choices to vote for, that is a large part of the problem. If you actually thought that either one of the remaining contestants was a good choice to lead your country or even just be the face of your nation then I have to either question your intelligence, your moral compass or both. It has been my experience so far that both generally tend to be the case.

I know very few things for certain: 1 - believe everything from no one, 2 - the most important truth is being true to yourself, and 3 - it's hard to argue with 2 + blue = hotdog (you can't rationalize with an irrational person). I have a few more but those are the main ones. I do know that a lot of the choices that were made for us at one time turn 180 degrees and we have to make those choices for someone else. When we have a child, we make choices for them that will, no doubt, change them from the person they would've been had we not bestowed that decision upon them. I know that we question many things, but I would have to agree for the most part with, the always inspirational, Wookiefoot who said, "If love is not the answer, then we just asked the wrong question". Because if we truly love, the other questions don't weigh as heavily.

That is the very reason that I think it is mental abuse to tell your children that you know the answers to the universe. If your answer to their question of, "how did we get here" doesn't start with, " I don't know" then you are lying to them and you are the problem. Religion isn't the problem. The problems are the idiots that believe and perpetuate it by brainwashing their children and the sick fucks that use it for control and domination in the name of their god (which is essentially the same thing). No one believes exactly the same thing. Even if you believe in god, you believe in it in a different way than anyone else does. The end result may be the same name, but there are many differences within that belief.

Just like two people imagining an old truck by a pond in front of a barn, do you think that if you could see both of their thoughts that every blade of grass, piece of the truck, board on that barn or cat tail by that pond would look the same? No, because people are different and think differently because of it. This is why two like-minded believers get different things from the very same sermon. They may get the same gist, but the intricacies are guaranteed to vary. Even a sermon delivered of the same scripture, by a different priest of the same faith, could not be the same as any other's because of their own personal differences and interpretations. How could you expect it to be any different for someone's thoughts or interpretations of the "thing that created it all"? Hell, the Christians don't even agree with the other Christians or, god forbid, those old testament thumpers that read from the same book. How could it be expected that they wouldn't unleash their unwillingness to follow their own "beliefs" in the form of wars on other factions to this day. It is, after all, the way that it became so widespread in the first place (can you say crusades), as is the case with almost every other religion.

I don't know who said it, but I am going to paraphrase it, regardless, because it is too on point to not; religion is like a penis. It is fine for you to have one and even to be proud of it but don't take it out in public, don't force it on children, don't force it down other's throats, don't make laws with it and don't think with it. I don't know that a more perfect comparison has ever been made. The one thing that I am the surest of is that there are some things that I will never know, no matter how hard I try, and I'm o.k. with that.

Life isn't always pretty and it is far from fair. This is a fact that we have to come to terms with if we are going to hope to be a contender in this fight. Even in the declaration of independence you aren't promised happiness, but the pursuit of it. That pursuit is a fight that you may not win. There are obstacles in the way of that happiness, the biggest of which is usually someone else's happiness. There will always be people who are made happy by your misfortunes. They aren't even always the bad guy. Sometimes you are just in the wrong place at the right time and get crushed under the wheels of great intentions. There are also birth defects, mental disabilities, social economic issues and weather. There are destructive leaders such as some parents, teachers, clergymen, presidents and kings. There are people that are just bad people and even just bad strokes of luck. Not all of us are going to make it out happily and none will get out alive but that doesn't mean that it is not worth the fight.

Being a good person does not guarantee you happiness but that isn't why you should work to be one. You should be a good person because it is the right thing to do, not for a reward. Alternatively, being a bad person doesn't necessarily mean that good things won't happen to you, or that you won't be happy. It may be your own warped twisted version of happy, but it is still happiness to you.

Granted, these are not the rule, but they happen too often for me to call them exceptions. They happen because of the biggest rule of them all: Life isn't fair. It can take you on a fantastic journey just to arrive at the best vantage point to see the worst thing you could ever possibly imagine and then push you right off the cliff, and laugh. Life can be almost as beautiful as it can be cruel. Love everything you can while you can. All we have is that beauty and it is everywhere, so soak it up because you can bet everything you have in the tank and the bank that the pain is coming, in one form or another.

Some people will never experience love or beauty. Whether it be from being born addicted to the mother's habit, a debilitating disease, into a home full of hate or just bad luck, accidents and natural disasters. However, every single person is born with the absolutely guaranteed promise of inescapable pain. It is a true fact of life. I don't necessarily think that it is good, but I do think that it is necessary. It must be of some importance to be so prevalent in everything we see. This thought is reinforced by how intertwined it is with the things we find the most enjoyable. We love to watch videos of people experiencing pain, we fall in and out of love in spite of it and perpetuate the cycle even further with pets and offspring. It is almost as if we can't truly live, or at least fully appreciate life without it. We need to accept this fact of life to thoroughly enjoy this life. Life is pain, but it is also the beauty that you may find along the way. The laughter, wonder, love and everything else that is the cause of our joy is what makes the pain worth it. Trying to constantly be better than yourself, learning to love when you thought you couldn't and helping out who you can on the way are three ways to take some of the sting out of that pain and to help make your journey even more fantastic.

 If we keep handing out participation trophies, rounding all of the sharp edges and telling our children that anything is possible for everyone or that prayer will stop the bad things, then we are doing the future generations a serious injustice. We are doing this by taking away the very tools that they will need to ever have a chance at being happy. This is not to say that you shouldn't try things because others think that it isn't possible. You should try anything that you think is possible and even some things that you think are not. There are many examples of things that, at one time, were thought to be impossible until someone did them (flight, space travel, summiting Mt. Everest, etc.). For reasons such as this I tend to agree, for the most part, with Henry Ford who said, "If you think that you can do a thing, or think you can't, you're right". I say, "for the most part" because you can't waste your life trying to complete a task that is actually impossible or it will have been just that, a waste.

Acceptance that something is impossible for you but possible for someone else, as well as even not possible for anyone, is key to understanding the truth. For example, being a man, I am not able to become pregnant, it is impossible, so I searched out a mate with the correct inner workings for whom it was possible. Had I tried with all of my heart, for all of my life to do it by myself I would have died without knowing my child.

Therefore, knowing what you can't do, can lead you on to the things that you were meant to do, or to things that you find truly fulfilling. Not getting a trophy when you didn't do a good job is what motivates you to do a better job next time. Seeing the girl that you think is not as smart as you get all of the flash card answers before you do is what shows you, for one, maybe you weren't the smarter one, and two, you have some work to do in the flash card department. Not having to deal with the bumps, bruises, bullies and even the shit hitting the fan despite their best efforts, along with not being told the truth, is what will keep them from ever being able to do any of them.

EDUTAINMENT AND ACCEPTANCE

Education is another choice that is made for us in the beginning. Our parents, teachers and clergy, to name a few, give us their interpretation of the knowledge that they have received. A lot of it is very useful, but a lot of it is exactly what keeps us all from getting along. We teach our kids everything from who to root for, to the flag to pledge your allegiance to, to hating people because of their color, accent, religion, music or even sexual preference and wonder why we can't get along. It is beyond me that so many "intelligent" people fall victim to victimizing their own children in the same way with the same unintelligent thought processes.

Stereotypes are a form of education that we get from an early age. They are basically the collection of mankind's accounts of millions of years of observation. I don't see how that cannot be used to our benefit. Some will argue that they are of no use but I find that a hilariously misguided attempt at political correctness. Stereotypes became stereotypes for a reason. That's because, for the most part, that tends to be the case. If you don't use stereotypes to help yourself navigate everyday situations you are not using a very beneficial tool. On the other hand, if you use them as the sole basis for judging a situation and treat them as a steadfast rule, you are misusing what has now become a violently destructive weapon.

If, for instance, you see a black man run really fast and then jump really high to dunk a basketball and you are blown away by the fact, then you didn't use one of your tools (stereotypes). If, however, you think that just because a man is black that he has to be able to do those things, then you, my friend, are wielding that violently destructive weapon. You can't be guffawed by the fact that the Asian child is good at math but you just as easily shouldn't expect it to be the case. In other words, if you aren't allowing them to be a part of your decision-making process then you are disregarding useful information. If you are using them as your primary decision-making factors, you are not using them as intended and are therefore doing yourself and others a disservice. It's just like when you hear the thunder, you can almost bet that the rain is coming. But don't be surprised if it doesn't, because that happens too. Plan for both.

They say, don't judge a book by its cover but you can normally gain some idea of the contents by doing just that. You do have to keep your mind open to the fact that there may be something different on the pages in between, but I've never opened up a children's book with a cute little duck on the cover and expected to see hard core porn. That doesn't mean that it couldn't happen but it sure would be quite a surprise. It would be a detriment to logic and to yourself to equally expect to see dicks or ducks when you open that book. You have to take the cover into account or you are not using all of the information at your disposal. There are such things as a hooker with a heart of gold, a stripper that's working her way through school to be a rocket scientist, freakishly fast fat people, corporate lobbyists that care about the little guy and even fish that can breathe on land but these are not generally the case. If you can't accept this and go into it expecting these to be the case, then expect to be wrong…. a lot.

 A number of women have a problem with the acceptance of the word, man, in the title of their employment. I didn't know this was a thing until I heard people bitching about it when I was a kid. I had never even given any thought to the word "man" in fireman meaning male, that females couldn't do it, or that they would be offended by it, up until then. I guess because I always thought that mankind included women. I thought that we called it mankind because of the word human (hu-man-kind). I thought that is why males are called man and females wo-man, because we are both hu-man. I never really thought about it, but once I did all I wondered was, "what will we call them now"? Do we just call them wo? Are they making up a new name? Will we have to change mankind and human now? Are we changing female too because of the male inference? Does the Spanish speaking contingent have the same problem with senor and senorita? Where the hell will this end? But then I remembered that the ones that are bitching about these names are the reason that it's called bitching. Don't worry, it's not a sexist thing, I think that the ones bitching up a storm about being called male nurses are equally as senseless.

In America we institutionalize our children rather than educate them. We compartmentalize, disassociate and standardize our education system to expect every different shaped peg to fit through the same hole. That is exactly what you want in an industrial world where being the manager of the local factory's assembly line is the goal. Living in a society that has changed so dramatically since the education system that we know today was devised, you would expect the education system to do the same to keep pace. If it weren't for the special interest groups, bureaucracy and the intention to not educate too much, I believe that the efforts of the ones that do care wouldn't be made in vain.

Even if the system were not the problem, the antiquated, falsified and laughable content of some of the information that we are giving them is exactly that. If you want to control someone you don't want to give them too many options, but a happier prisoner thinks that he has some. You definitely can't give them too much knowledge because knowledge is power, but just to make sure, you better not allow them to acquire much wealth either. Too much of any of these makes someone very hard to control. So, you control what they are taught (schools and churches), you control what they see (television, newspapers, etc.) and you control the money (Federal Reserve, International Monetary Fund, World Bank etc.). End of story.

It doesn't matter if it is one person or thousands, if you're not one of them and as long as they are on the same page, you're screwed. Why wouldn't they be on the same page? It would be good for profits and sustainability of said profits if they were on the same page, correct? You do the math.

In the 8th grade I figured out that the president is just the equivalent of the principal of the school. Yes, they may be able to affect your daily life somewhat, but they do not set the agenda. Earlier in my schooling, the teacher had a little bit of power, at least in the form of paddling (taking that away, from the schools and parents, is partly to blame for the problems with this generation). Other than that, I found that the teacher doesn't really have any power to speak of. They have to go to the principal who has a very limited amount of power as well, being that they must now confer with the super-intendant. The super-intendant gets his orders from the school board, you know, the parents of the kids that suck but are somehow starting for the basketball team. These are the people that you never hear about but that have the money and the clout to steer the super- intendant in their desired direction. The rules that they all must adhere to are state or federally mandated.

The reason that these other entities are involved are power and profit based. Anytime there is money and or power at stake, we as humans will find a way to fight about it. In much the same way, I realized that the government is no different. The president is no more than a puppet. The right and the left just signify the two hands of the elite that pull the strings. To be the president you must be a morally corrupt yes man for the powers that be. No more than a face or name to put on the problem (Obamacare, Trumptaxplan, etc.) so as not to, themselves (elite), have to answer to the peons.

If you don't think that there is an "elite" ruling class, just research some of the old boy's clubs and special interest groups that most of the presidents, high ranking cabinet members, CEOs and other leaders of industry belong to. Tell me what you think after you do your due diligence and read about institutions such as the Trilateral Commission, Council on Foreign Relations, Skull and Bones, Bilderberg Group and Bohemian Grove. Compare the lists of their members with the fucksticks that have been, are now and will be in power for the foreseeable future.

These people make decisions that affect millions of lives on a daily basis but they are just the people that work for the ones that have the real wealth, which equals true power. Billionaires are laughed at as wanna-bes by this crowd. You don't hear their names for a reason, and they are the "elite". When you do, it is because of their philanthropy no doubt. Rothschilds, Rockefellers, Warburgs, Morgans and others like them are rarely heard from in anything other than a positive context unless you're listening to those damn conspiracy theorists. If you're not listening to them, maybe you should start.

A person that wants to truly change things for the people's best interest can't be allowed in office because they might actually change things. They wouldn't want things like their 100 dollar pens, 1000 dollar hammers, band aid research programs and corporate lobbying to disappear, now would they? Do you think that the manufacturers of weapons of war or their stockholders hope for peace? Hell no, and neither do the people that stand to gain from the resources that those wars are fought over (usually the same people). The principal may be allowed to tell you not to run in the halls but he doesn't have control over where and how those walls are built, let alone the power to decide what is taught between them. That power comes from the people with the money.

In the case of who makes the agenda, as in any investigation, you follow the money. You only have to look as far as who stands to gain, and from what, to figure most things out. Whether you think it is banking cartels, corporations, special interest groups, corrupt government officials, arms manufacturers and dealers or elites that want to stay that way then you are probably right. But my guess would be that it's a little bit of all of them. I don't know that there is one world boss, a board or a collective but you can bet your ass that the centuries old saying of, "give me control of a nations money and I care not who makes its laws" holds true to this very day.

The 2016 election was just a test to see exactly how bought off, ignorant and entertained the American people are. It pains me to see how miserably "we the people" failed that test. You failed no matter who you voted for. The choices given to us were almost as deplorable as the ruse to make you think that your vote matters in the first place (bush election 2004). The person that they wanted to win won or that person wouldn't be alive, it really is as simple as that. It is this illusion of choice that they are selling, and most of you can't seem to buy enough of it.

Either way, if you give me the choice between a cold shit sandwich and a warm shit sandwich I have the brains to decline tonight's dinner and wait until a more appetizing dish becomes available. If the kitchen keeps offering such shitty choices because of its inattention to the ingredients, then I would call for a change of staff. If that doesn't work, we tear that sucker down and build a better one in its place. I'm pretty sure that it doesn't even call it your right in the constitution, but your duty. (ha-ha I said duty)

If we really wanted to make changes, we would stop paying government officials such exorbitant salaries along with stopping those payments at the end of their term instead of paying it to them for the rest of their lives. A doctor that saves lives should stop being payed when they retire but a senator that takes bribes should not? If, along with this, we started taxing the churches we would have free health care and free college education. If it didn't get us all the way there I'm sure it would knock off an American, super-sized portion of it. These aren't monies that would have to be raised, they are funds that are being left on the table or misappropriated as we speak. Or, in layman's terms, they are just being spent on the wrong shit.

 I'm not necessarily a fan of the free health care system in the VA and free clinic models we see implemented today. I do however think that some system of it could be devised to better put this money to use. It would be better still to not have this money stolen from us in the first place in the form of income tax. This is a large part of what has created the cofuckingnundrum that we are in now. It is also one of the things that will keep us from having the freedom that we all profess to have such a yearning for. This topic deserves more attention and is covered more thoroughly in my next book (We, the people that give a shit...).

 If we truly want change, we would hold government officials and corporate fat cats accountable for defrauding, misinforming and stealing from the people. We should then send them to the same hellish privatized prison system that they've helped create and have them treated no differently than any other inmate.

As long as we are really making changes, then I guess we would have to re-think that whole privatization model when it is concerning the military or the prison complex (Blackwater, Northbridge Services Group, Core civic, GEO Group). It is a model that both have proven to be far too damaging to the people they profess to help and far too profitable to these private companies for them to give up without one hell of a fight.

We'd flip lawyer's and teacher's salaries and expect more out of both. We'd stop paying entertainers millions of dollars to be "role models" for our kids and start paying attention to the kids and what we are really teaching them and maybe we would become those role models. Wouldn't that just be too logical?

Entertainment is a very good distraction and we have used it since our days in the caves drawing pictures, making music and telling stories around the fire. Sometimes we used it out of boredom and sometimes to keep our mind off of other pressing issues. Sometimes we did it because everyone else was doing it and other times we did it just because it was fun. Most of our time, however, was spent surviving. We have found many more ways to entertain ourselves over the years and the availability of those forms of entertainment have increased exponentially. Along with that, we now live in houses and have grocery stores, telephones and electricity, so we aren't quite as busy surviving.

Now, if a person isn't interested for more than 3 seconds, they have to change the channel, video game, chat room, app, device, social media, toy, or whatever other screen they have glued to their face and tweet, post, selfie or blog about it. We are very entertained and we intend to stay that way. It doesn't matter if we don't put out as many theoretical physicists and rocket scientists as long as we get to see the game or who won "America's got "me" issues", right? Why worry about school levies, taxes or teacher's salaries when you could be helping to pay a baseball player 500,000 dollars every Friday for playing a game?

 Why worry about the idiots that are in power around you and actually do something about it when you could just watch Game of Thrones and talk shit? Why truly care, "accept" and help people when you can just say a prayer, post a ribbon or drop some coin in the plate after the hymns? Unfortunately, these cases are all too prevalent due primarily to the fact that being entertained is much more fun and a lot less work than caring and doing something about a problem. It's not entertainment's fault, it's yours for satisfying your greedy human urges rather than thinking of the future of your children or the world.

 Of the many forms of entertainment, religion has to be one of the most destructive and lucrative. The different religions, just different broadcasting companies vying for their piece of the ratings. Each company puts out a variety of programs (churches, mosques, temples, synagogues, etc.) and each has their own unique set and host with their own unique style and interpretation of the script (scriptures). There are even bake sales and games, gatherings for rejoice and mourning, singing, dancing and even the news (who died, who went to jail for pedophilia, etc.). There are also telethons (give me your money) and bingo!!! just like tv.

 The biggest thing that religion entertains is our need for answers to why we are here and what happens after this. It is a much simpler explanation, and I have to admit, that I would sure love to truly believe that my compassionate creator made me in his image and that I get to reunite with all of my loved ones (the ones that made the cut) and the creator and live in peace for eternity after I die. Unfortunately, intelligence, simple math and no need to follow the flock keep me from placing much stock in such drivel. Add to that a huge amount of distrust for anyone that says that they know the answer to why we are here or how we got here and you get right back to my "I don't know"...... and neither do you.

 No one can tell me that everything had to be created and then argue that their creator is the only exception to that rule (without getting a well-deserved laugh). If it didn't have to be created and was just there from the beginning, then one could easily argue that any of the other things that exist didn't need to be created and could have just been there from the beginning. In the same way, no one can tell me that what created everything was a big bang. In order for there to be a big bang there had to have already been two things that existed that could bang together and where did they come from? The reason that no one can tell me is because no one was around to see it happen or even existed (in the form that we know) until millions of years later (less in other beliefs). Even then you are talking about someone making their best guess and then passing it down through that gigantic game of telephone. Add to that, some people's suspect intentions, and it makes it that much less believable.

Still yet, people continue watching these "programs" (subscribing to religious beliefs) no matter what part of their core it is entertaining. In doing so, they make the choice to be entertained by that belief and to believe that everyone else is wrong, and that doesn't usually end well. Some people don't believe as steadfastly as others but continue watching because they like the cast or the show and just feel that it is better than watching the alternative programming. If you don't question that choice and belief constantly and probe other areas for truths, then programming is the perfect word for it.

I heard something in a corporate acceptance training seminar one day that sounded like the rest of the gibberish that they pour down your throat as if they care about it at all, but this was different. It would have seemed more genuine had the company not been forced to put on seminars such as this by a judge after being found guilty of racial inequality. Regardless, there was a nugget of wisdom to be gained from their mistake and along with it I got paid for not working for an hour, so I call it a win.

The wisdom nugget was this: don't treat others the way you want to be treated, treat them the way they want to be treated. This is different from the conventional wisdom but I believe it to be a much better solution to what could easily become a problem otherwise. Treating someone like you want to be treated is a very selfish (human) way to think about things. If this is the case, then you would have to be o.k. with the self-destructive guy on the bus that likes to burn himself with his cigar walking up to you and burning you with his cigar. It is, after all, the way he wants to be treated. I like to keep that nugget in mind when interacting with others so that we are all as happy as possible, but if for nothing else, just to keep my conscience clean when I hit that guy on the bus in the face for burning me with his cigar.

As different as my beliefs are from others, I don't attack them because of it. Retaliation, though, is definitely an option depending on the threat. I am accepting of the fact that there are others that believe differently than I do, and that they may very well be right and I am wrong. I don't think that I have all of the answers. This is only the result of the way that I have processed the information that I have encountered and the way that it makes me feel. That is all anyone's thoughts or beliefs are. We are all very different and expect those differences to be accepted. Those differences are harder for some people to deal with, and that is a difference of theirs that you need to accept if you expect the same for yours.

Whether I like something or not is of no matter to me until it directly infringes on my human rights. There are people that think that orange is the best color in the world and who am I to disagree with what they think is the best? I can disagree with the fact that "I" think it is the best, but not that it is the one that "they" think is the best. I am fine with them loving it, wearing it, eating it and even painting their house orange (no matter how hideous I may think it is). I don't have a problem until you try to tell me or my kids that their life should be orange or I come home and find you painting my house. I am accepting up until that point.

George Orwell said, "happiness can only happen through acceptance" and for the most part, I would agree. I believe that acceptance is key but not at all costs. I understand that people have differences, wants, needs and beliefs but if you think, want, need or believe that it's ok to rape and kill children, I can't and won't accept that. There are times that acceptance is not the right answer and that is one of them. There are many examples of times that it is not the right answer but they are heavily outweighed by the times that it is. I make the choice to be accepting until the point that it violates the rights, wellbeing or life of me, mine or anyone else I am aware of and even those I'm not. I'm not saying that it's right, it's just the choice that I've made.

One thing that we have a hard time accepting is getting older, even though it is the most unavoidable thing that we all face. My head is like America and my reddish-brown hairs are like the Indians. A few whites have found their way in and they just keep bringing or making more. Soon enough they will choke out most of the indigenous color and there will be nothing but a few stragglers on reservations (my nose and ears). I hope I at least get a casino out of the deal.

Still, people do everything they can to try to keep from feeling older, or looking like it anyway, like coloring their hair, Botox injections and wonder pills. Along with better nutrition, sanitation and medical attention, we have made medical advancements and even replacement parts to squeeze as much out of these mortal coils as possible. The result is a population of geriatrics that is larger than it has ever been before and it shows no sign of stopping anytime soon. America's 65 and over population is expected to almost double between now and 2050 from 48 million to 88 million. The world's "oldest" population (80+) is expected to grow by 300% over the next few decades in most of the world and even by 400% in others. This is going to put our healthcare and economic systems to the test in more ways than one (transportation, housing, pensions, disability, poverty, Medicaid, social security). It seems as if we just don't want to stop until someone else has to wipe our ass for us again. I don't know anybody that is happy about death, myself included, but I'm going to use these years in between diapers to their fullest so that when I do have to wear them again, and they are at their fullest, I can at least revel in the memories (barring Alzheimer's or dementia).

IGNORANCE AND IDIOSYNCRASIES

There is a big difference between dumb, stupid and ignorant. Dumb is not having the tools to deal with the problem. It is when someone lacks the mental capacity but not necessarily the physical abilities to deal with a situation. Dumb is not being able to get it, no matter how much you want to, or how good the teacher is or how many times you try (with the exception of blind luck).

Dumb, I can deal with because I've found that, for the most part, they mean well and I generally know what to expect from them. Stupid on the other hand is something altogether different and is a thing that I have a much harder time dealing with. Stupid is when you have all of the tools at your disposal but you decide to use them in the wrong way, or not to use them at all. It's knowing that you need a saw but deciding to use your head to cut the board instead and then trying to drive a hammer into it with a nail. Stupid is understanding every piece of information and disregarding it intentionally for your own fucked up reasoning.

I am lucky enough to not fall into the dumb category. I have, however, done some stupid things. I don't think that I fall into the stupid category because I have learned from those stupid mistakes and work diligently to not repeat them (except smoking). I do fall into the ignorant category with astute regularity, as do we all. Ignorance is the lack of knowledge or information and there isn't anyone on this planet that can argue that they are without ignorance. To do so would be to profess that you know everything that there is to know about everything. Even I know that only a fool has all of the answers. There are millions of things that I am not ignorant of, maybe even billions but there is not a number that exists that could come close to representing the countless things that I am ignorant of. I do think that this is the first step to enlightenment and knowledge because if you think that you know everything then you think that there is nothing to learn. Or, to loosely quote Ram Daas; "if you think you're free, then you can't escape".

Ignorance is nothing to be ashamed of as long as you are willing to use the new tools and knowledge that you find along the way to become less ignorant. Ignorance is a thing that we all have in common, except for the quantity of it, and is not a bad thing as long as you're willing to learn. Some people decide, for whatever reason, to remain ignorant. They refuse to look any further than they have already been led, and in this form, it is no longer ignorance, but stupidity. Avoiding the knowledge does not make it cease to exist, it just keeps you from being able to use it or to grow from it. In the process, I've found that I wouldn't call myself wise. I might call myself fallible, loving, rational, truthful or observant, and if I died only being able to claim those, I would be a happy man but I will always be ignorant of more than I'm not.

Sometimes ignorance can be a gigantic problem. In America people put the country's forefathers on a pedestal (even though they were sexist and racist) as if they are beyond reproach. The very same people disregard the actual history in favor of their storybook vision and claim to be loyalists. It's odd because they are willing to go to war to spread democracy. This is strange because democracy is a historically poor excuse for freedom, unless you are in the majority. It is a system that allows 51% of the people to take away 49% of the peoples' rights. It is also a system that was despised by the men that they so revere (I love unintended puns). The forefathers did have their issues but they were right to not like democracy. That is precisely why we are not supposed to be one, we are supposed to be a constitutional republic. This is why you pledge, "and to the republic for which it stands" not " and to the democracy….". In a constitutional republic you are not allowed to make a law that infringes on anyone's rights (accept maybe the natives, women, non-landowning men, and anybody that wasn't white) even if the vote is

97

99 to 1. It is a much more credible, but not by any means, perfect system.

The same ignorance is blatantly apparent if you flip through the main stream news networks or your favorite social media platform. You will hear people propping up their party as if it does no wrong while the other side argues back with the same obliviousness. Both spewing hate and, most of the time, factually incorrect arguments. This is exactly why there are separate parties, to keep us divided. They know that if everybody got on the same page or at least realized at all that they don't have a choice, that we would be a force that they would be powerless to stop. It is called divide and conquer for a reason and we are making it far too easy for them by picking up what they're putting down faster than they can drop it like it's hot. We are just that little kid in the audience at a magic show being fooled by the misdirection (arguing) of the magician's stealthy hands (right and left) or the distraction of his beautiful assistant (illusion of choice). A lot of people are starting to see the wires and question the, not so real looking feet, hanging out of the box. Some are even appalled enough by the blatant fuckery that they are getting up, walking out and demanding their money back. Still, far too many are paying through the nose to be front and center for the next show. Maybe Ignorance is bliss.

I hear people on social media, television and even at thanksgiving dinner make comments about all of these degenerates getting welfare being one of the more important economic challenges that we face. I absolutely agree that it is a problem but probably not in the way that you think. Franny food stamps, buying steaks, pop and chips and collecting checks for all 6 of her kids, living on section8 while checking her iphone8, is a problem that needs to be addressed, yes. But it is 2% of the "welfare" problem in this country. 98% of what falls under the "welfare" umbrella is corporate welfare. Companies like Walmart, Coca Cola, GE, IBM and Halliburton that make millions/billions in profits and still receive millions/billions in subsidies, tax breaks and welfare. These are people that are being driven places in their Bentley, eating gold covered truffles dipped in caviar, living in mansions and vacationing in one of their homes in; insert opulent destination here, while being handed hundreds of thousands to billions of dollars a year in government kickbacks (welfare). Franny food stamps doesn't seem like as much of a problem with her busted up civic pulling up to her stoop in the projects now does she?

 Still yet, you will have a, not so mentally proficient, portion that will condemn welfare of any kind calling it socialism. They say this as if caring and helping people less fortunate should be a punishable offense. I highly doubt that, if their house was on fire, that their first call would be to a neighbor with a garden hose, but rather to the fire department (a socialist program). I believe that it would be much the same if they were robbed or needed to find information or a book. The police department and libraries also rely heavily or solely on federal funding. I am not for more government being involved in our everyday lives because of lobbying special interest groups, crooked, self-serving politicians and the refusal, by the powers that be, to prosecute those that take part in these activities. This doesn't mean that I am against helping those in need that can't afford it. On the contrary, I am all for it, providing the parties are deserving of the help and appreciative of it rather than manipulating it for their own benefit. Oh yeah, and the fact that they actually need it helps too.

 Ignorance can sometimes be the cause of the idiosyncrasies and mannerisms that we see in each other. For instance, I find it funny that people bless you when you sneeze, and that it happens in almost every country. There are many reasonings for it (none of them sane). Some think you sneeze because evil spirits are leaving your body while others think that it is when evil enters the body. Others believe that your heart stops when you sneeze and the bless you is welcoming you back to life. The German word gesundheit means health, while Hindus, Russians and the Chinese have responses to a sneeze that mean, essentially, the same thing. I still think it is funny that out of all of the bodily expulsions, the sneeze gets this special consideration of others blessing you or wishing you well. On the other hand, you are supposed to apologize or excuse yourself after a cough, burp or fart. If there was a time that someone might think there were evil spirits leaving the body, I know which one I'd be blessing instead of the sneeze. Most people don't say it for any of those reasons now. When I ask people why they say it, I normally get the "common courtesy" or "manners" explanation but it only makes it funnier to me because they don't care about either of those when I cough, burp or fart. Does that make them bodily functionists? I think so. I say bless them all or none. No function left behind!

Words can be a powerful weapon that lift people up and give them hope but that can just as easily tear them down and leave them feeling hopeless. It is not the words that have the power but the meaning behind them that give them their validity and might. Take what we consider today to be vulgar or offensive words, these have changed through the years and through the miles that they have travelled. Fag is considered an offensive word here and today but if you ask for a fag in England or even here 200 years ago you would've been given a cigarette, not an effeminate man. The word didn't change, but the meaning did. In much the same way, if you asked for a cock while strolling by the chicken coop you would probably end up with something very different than if you asked for the same thing while standing in an alley in the Castro district in San Francisco.

The meaning of words such as shit, cunt, goddamn, and my absolute favorite and most versatile word ever, fuck, can change dramatically, even within the same sentence, depending on the intent of the distributor. I do not view them as lesser words by any stretch of the imagination and there are none better to express my feelings at some points. To use any other word at these times would be convoluting or at least overthinking, not to mention not being true to what I meant. I challenge you to find a word that can be used in so many ways to mean so many different things as the word fuck. I believe it to be the most versatile word known to man. I do not view words such as these, for myself anyway, as hiding holes in my vocabulary game as much as being used for effect that cannot be achieved with any other word.

Even though there are many words to describe fire, if I had to do it with one, I would use the word hot. I could have used blazing to be more descriptive of the temperature, illuminating for its light or been more vague and philosophical and said vivification, but none of these would have gotten to the core of explaining it to the biggest selection of people as would the word hot. Therefore, the best one word to describe fire is hot. Why use a different one? To seem smarter, better, more descriptive? Might that not get my message across as clearly to as wide of an audience? Sometimes the best word is just the best word (providing it is an appropriate setting).

The people that find words like these offensive, generally have their own set of words that they use in place of these words. For example; work ate my lunch today instead of work kicked my ass today. This may suffice as a separate phrase for a day that wasn't quite as hard, but not in place of kicked my ass. At the end of the day, would you feel better if someone ate your lunch or kicked your ass? So, if today kicked your ass but you say ate my lunch instead, maybe you aren't being honest with yourself (unless you are diabetic).

 Sometimes it is as simple as calling a pile of shit a less offensive, widely accepted term such as poop or by changing the word slightly and using fudge instead of fuck when you stub your toe. Either way, the word may have changed but the meaning behind the word was the same. In the case of the stubbed toe, wouldn't ouch have been a more correct term to use than fudge? By saying fudge, all you are doing is changing the word fuck, you aren't changing the meaning of what you were trying to express which ouch, obviously wasn't quite strong enough of a word for. I would argue that it is just trying to cheat the system. If you were truthful, you would say that you meant "FUCK" but you didn't want to say the word or weren't allowed. If what you mean is one thing but you say another, I consider this a lie. It is a lie to yourself, to the person that you're speaking to and to the deity, society or parent that made you think that it was a bad word in the first place. You still mean the same thing, you are just trying to hide it by rearranging a few letters.

 I am actually more offended by people going out of their way to not use foul language than someone that overuses it and even more by those that are offended by it and complain. Why shouldn't my being offended matter just as much as theirs, especially if I am the one being honest?

 If you repeatedly stab a person in the belly while telling them you love them, what would a bystander be more likely to believe, your words or your blood drenched blade? Words do not change actions but actions can absolutely change words. If I tell my child to go to their room and they stomp up the stairs saying, "love you dad, you're the best" in an abrasive, sarcastic or disrespectful tone, they get grounded. Their actions changed the words. I know what they meant, they just didn't want to say it because they feared repercussions because of the words, but the words that they used couldn't hide how they truly felt. The disrespect is what is punishable, not the word. Fuck you dad, you're a piece of shit, wouldn't have been punished any more severely. As a matter of fact, I would probably show more lenience in that case because of the truthfulness of not trying to hide their feelings behind different words. I tend to side with Dr. Seuss on this matter, when he said, "be who you are and say what you feel, because those who mind don't matter and those that matter don't mind"

 Words can be misinterpreted, misunderstood or just not known at all. All of these can lead to conflict which might not have happened if the feeling had been conveyed in a more understandable way. Sometimes being so vague that they may be perceived differently by different individuals is precisely the intent. You don't have to look farther than the bible's scriptures, Nostradamus' quatrains or the horoscope section of your favorite rag for shining examples of this. Not that words are unimportant, but they do tend to get in the way of the truth from time to time. The written language isn't the perfect way to communicate but that does not change how powerful it is. I'm sure that we will find a better way eventually.

Until then, I call myself white, not because that is the actual color of my skin but because it is the term that is widely known to describe a person with my skin tone. I will, in turn, call black people black and the American Indian, Indians (unless specifically asked not to by the individual). These are not terms of disrespect but of widely used and mostly agreed upon terms of identification. The word brunette isn't an offensive term used to describe people with brown hair, it's just the common reference. If you are offended by it, maybe you are just too easily offended or just looking for a reason to be. If this is the case and your being offended offends me then shouldn't you be the one that should stop? Or maybe you just need to be offended, and if that's the case I will be more than happy to oblige. I try not to offend anyone out of sheer respect but I am sick of the politically correct hoops that you have to jump through these days to keep this entitled, thin-skinned, built-to-whine movement happy.

I'm sure that there were other names on the list when deciding on the word green for the crayon. But green is the name that was agreed upon or at least that stuck. I wouldn't invest in a statue, though, because that seems to be the offensive medium that pushes people over the edge. It's probably only still called green because of so little uproar from the chlorophyll community. I'm sure it's days are numbered. My point is, that there are different names on all of those colors of crayons, they are not disrespectful and are there for a reason. That reason is identification. If we keep changing the names on the paper, I can't easily explain which colors I used and you would have a much harder time trying to replicate or attain those same colors.

If there are 4 people that you have never met in a room, a black guy, a white guy, a Chinese girl, and a red-headed Irish girl and I send you in to give a message to one of them specifically, I need to describe them to you. If I tell you that it is for the black guy, it has nothing to do with being offensive but everything to do with the fact that he is the only black person in the room.

If I say it is for the Asian girl, it isn't a derogatory statement. I just don't know exactly which country from that area of the globe her ancestors inhabit and neither do you, but we both know who I am talking about. My son is half Korean, Korea is in Asia, therefore, my son is half Asian. It's not offensive, it's math. If you know that his ancestors were from Korea then feel free to call him half Korean instead, that's great. I don't even mind the term oriental. If you look up the definition of the word (of, from or characteristic of east Asia) you would find that it perfectly describes the origin and is not derogatory in the least. If you find it offensive, then you are probably one of the ones that are too easily offended and that is your problem and lack of understanding, not mine.

If I say that the message is for the red headed girl or the white girl it isn't meant to offend anyone that I didn't call her Irish, I just didn't know where she was from. We could, however, both see that she has red hair and is white so it should be easy to understand why I would use either of those. In the same way, if the white guy were wearing a sombrero I would just tell you to give it to the one wearing the sombrero (or big hat if I didn't know its correct name). That is the same way that I would describe anyone that was wearing the hat, if that is who the message was for, because that would have been the easiest way for both of us to know who I was talking about.

People need to stop being offended by such trivial bullshit. It's just another reason to cry, "woe is me" and pretend that everything is aimed at them because they are the most important thing on anyone's mind. Get it through your narcissistically thick skull, it's not all about you! It's about us.

I know god fearing people that are offended by farts. Offended by the involuntary bodily function, and by the person in that body, not by the god that "invented" the fart. Get over it, get over yourself and just get along. Choose your battles more carefully than you choose your friends because it is exactly what will decide which you have more of. Quantity is not the goal for either case though. Quality should be the goal in these and just about all of the choices you will ever make.

ADDICTION &
CONTRADICTION

Addiction is a hell of a drug. We are all addicted to something. The first thing that comes to mind when you start thinking about addiction is drugs. This is definitely one of the heavy hitters. The definition of a drug is; any substance that when introduced to the body, causes a physiological change. Therefore, I would argue that just about anything in this world is a drug. Our body produces chemicals such as dopamine, serotonin, oxytocin and endorphins that make us happy for a number of reasons, such as when we see our children or complete a goal or any number of other events. These same chemicals are responsible for the "effects" of some drugs such as cocaine and ecstacy which, when taken, cause the brain to produce these chemicals. Some of these same chemicals are produced when you see an electronic screen (computer, television, phone, etc.) making screens, by definition, a drug.

People's addictions are as varied as their personalities. As detestable as you may find something, that may be the very thing that trips someone else's trigger. Serial killers would be a prime example. I've even seen a girl that was addicted to pee filled diapers. She would collect them from willing parents and smell them and even chew on them. Gross, right? She didn't think so, and that is my point. My roommate for a few years on the road, Ivan, is one that I always think about. His list of requirements for the most physically attractive woman in the world is exactly the same as the list of things that would make her the least physically attractive woman to me. Different strokes...

My wife likes salt and vinegar chips and I can't even be in the same room as an opened bag of them and this has since become the way that I view my differences with people. I don't like salt and vinegar chips but just because you do, doesn't mean that there aren't thousands of other things that we can agree on, or that we can't love each other despite our disagreeable differences.

People can be addicted to food to the point of being so fat that they have to tear down walls to remove them from their home. Is the food the problem? Should we make it illegal or at least regulate the amount you are allowed to have? Other people become addicted to things like money, tv, computers, coffee and porn. All of these things cause physiological changes when introduced, so are these things the problem? No, they are not the problem or everyone that experienced them would have fallen victim in much the same manner. The people in the situation are the problem. It is their lack of strength, willingness, will power, resolve and sometimes inherent chemical or physical reasons that makes them addicted. It is much the same for cars and even guns. These things elicit similar chemical responses in some people but the ones that are responsible and ethical along with mentally and chemically proficient are less likely to drive down the sidewalk mowing down pedestrians while gunning down toddlers in the park across the street. The guns and the cars aren't the problem or that is the way they would be used the majority of the time by the majority of the people and that is far from the case with either.

Addiction is not a disease. That is a way to try to rationalize a situation rather than face the truth. Addiction is a choice. Whether you are brainwashed, not mentally capable enough, too morally corrupt or just wired that way it is still a choice, not a disease. It is a disease in the way that lack of common sense and compassion are diseases today. As with these, addiction falls more into the category of a deficiency. A deficiency of self-control, critical thinking, will power and resolve. People practice religion, do drugs, eat food and use technology responsibly every day without becoming addicted to them to the point of mental collapse or death, but they decide to take part or continue to do so by choice. I don't disagree that any of these things can be absolutely deadly when abused and that, once introduced, one may be able to contort it enough to fit the "definition" of disease. People's perceptions of these definitions vary just like they do with scriptures, rights and instructions. They will try to bend and twist the word and definition to make it fit their way of thinking so that they can more easily explain the situation to themselves. The fact of the matter, though, is that you don't willingly choose to have or to continue to take part in AIDS, Alzheimer's, Ebola or any other true disease.

Some people say that drugs are a way to escape reality. I guess that can be true but I tend to think of them as a way to enhance reality. I would go one further to say that there isn't anyone that doesn't want their reality enhanced. No matter what it is, if you didn't pop out of your momma with it, it is enhancing your reality. Clothes and fire are just the drugs that we used to enhance our reality in the caves when that reality proved to be too cold for our liking. Almost all of us are addicted to this now in one way, shape or form. You can look in any direction right now and find a multitude of examples of the way that you are enhancing (escaping) your reality. Shoes, clothes, medicine, religions, vehicles, homes, electricity and tools along with millions of other items are all examples of things that you didn't have or grow when you were born. Therefore, they are enhancing the reality that you were born into. You were then introduced to these drugs and sometimes forced to use them but the choice to continue using them and in what manner is yours.

The misinformed, the brainwashed and the ones that it benefits monetarily to keep it illegal call marijuana a gateway drug. I find this absolutely hilarious just because simple mathematics tell us a much different story. I know as many or more people that smoke pot that have never tried other illegal drugs than I do heroin or crack users whose first drug was marijuana. There are just as many or more people that didn't like pot because it made them tired, laugh too much or paranoid, so they looked elsewhere. Just as many moved on because it was a stronger buzz than they were looking for as did because it wasn't strong enough.

Most drug users that I have met are unfortunately introduced to alcohol first, in large part, due to the fact that it is legal. I would still argue that even alcohol is not a gateway drug for the simple fact that many users of alcohol are happy to never try anything else because they are happy with that alcohol buzz. Yet again there are just as many illegal drug users that didn't try alcohol first, tried it and just didn't like it and those that have never tried it at all. There is no such thing as a gateway drug.

When you tried crayons, but they didn't color the picture the way you envisioned so you tried markers and they did, were crayons your gateway colors just because you tried them first and they didn't do the job? No, you were searching for a way to color a picture to fit your vision and you tried the first thing that you could find to do so. If you would have started with chalk, the image still would not have looked as you desired so you would have moved on to another medium until you found the one that achieved your objective. So, in essence, where you started doesn't matter nearly as much as where you "want" to end. If your vision was accomplished with the first medium, you wouldn't have moved on to markers and you wouldn't have stuck with markers had they not achieved that desired effect.

 If there is anything that is a gateway drug, meaning most that try it move on to other things, it would be breathing. It is the only thing that every drug user tried first and decided that it alone was not good enough and that they wanted more (something else). Where are the, "breath is death" adds? Whether it's ho-ho's, tofu, heroin, religion, stamps, power, work or any of the other things on this planet that can be abused, it is personal responsibility and self-control or the lack thereof, that make it a problem. Drugs aren't being abused, critical thinking and moderation are being abused. When you abuse these two things, you make a suspect decision and then do it too often, what do you expect? If you force the fruits of your labor down the wrong wolf's throat and stare at his hindsight until it shits in your spoon, then, yes, you have an eating problem, but more importantly, you have a thinking problem not a disease. The object is not the problem, people are. They always have been and they always will be. This whole drug section could have easily fallen into the accountability chapter:)

 One might argue that consumerism is one of the more dangerous drugs that is available. I would have to agree simply because it has been so engrained in our lives that it almost seems commonplace or even necessary. After 9/11, the U.S. government's advice to the public was not to gather and talk to each other about the issues, to grieve or to search for the truth or the real culprits. It was to shop! When the president tells you that you have to shop to save the country, it is a huge red flag that signifies that your government has already been bought. Bought by the idea that it is all; of the dollar, by the dollar, for the dollar, not the people.

It is easily seen every Christmas season when the ads and decorations start months in advance. They have to make sure you have time to cross everything off of your many lists of what everyone just has to have this year. We wouldn't want our children ridiculed for not wearing the newest pair of 100 dollar + sneakers or because their phone that still works perfectly isn't the latest version, now would we? If that were the case, then we would have to look into the eyes of any of the Jones' going by in their new model BMWs, using their sleek new computer or wearing the heels or jeans that are trending this year and try not to feel less significant ourselves. This is called perceived obsolescence. This is the reason that there is always a new version. It isn't because the version you have doesn't work well enough. It's because you may not feel the need to buy another version if yours works fine unless compelled by social stigma to do so. Thank you, commercials, for telling us that none of our shit is good enough.

You don't need to look any further than our landfills, oceans or even the side of the road to see the side effects of this toxic drug. We are creating waste at an alarming rate. 99 percent of the things we buy end up in the trash within 6 months!!!!!! Yes, that was six exclamation points and I would've had to hold the button down for months to come close to the tone of my feelings on the subject. Sickeningly enough, a lot of this is by design. After World War 2, corporations incorporated a system called planned obsolescence into the production of consumer goods. For the longest time, quality and longevity were the selling points that manufacturers hung their hats on. With this new system, products are intentionally designed to fail in a shorter amount of time as to prompt another purchase. How's that for caring about your best interest, or the planet for that matter?

We make the choice to buy these products, we do not need them. If we refused to buy said products until production practices and quality levels bettered, then they would have to listen to us and change their tactics or go out of business. If we cared less that the person next to us felt that we were inferior because of our older car, clothes or gadgets (perceived obsolescence) we wouldn't need to go buy the new versions. Just remember that it starts with you not being one of those people looking down your nose at your neighbor if you ever expect them to do the same. The power is ours, but we are choosing not to use it by continuing to accept such detrimental practices.

I think that Christmas is a great ambassador for consumerism because they mirror each other's twisted perspectives so neatly. Christmas is just an amalgamation of drunken parent's scare tactics (the original Christmas, Krampus), advertising agendas (Santa and sales), pagan rituals (yule log and stockings), Victorian snobbery (Christmas tree), bible stories (baby Jesus, 3 wise men, St. Nick) and reindeer games (Rudolph, elves, north pole). While consumerism is just the deformed child of corporations, advertisers and media that creepy uncle government likes to touch too much.

Contradictions can be as destructive as any addiction. They make us overlook the similarities that could tear down walls rather than build them. We let them divide us rather than unite us. We contradict ourselves regularly as a society every day without much thought about it at all. We do it with clothing when there are complaints of other cultures wearing head wraps. Whether it is a hijab, niqab, chador or burqa the question is; "how can they make their women cover themselves like that?" First of all, a lot of those women cover themselves by choice or for religious reasons. Second, I have been in public places in America where some obscenely obese guy sweats his way through the crowd flaunting his uncovered double ds while the law requires any female to cover the very same region of her own body. Hello pot, meet kettle. Third and finally, try to walk around the grocery store or the mall naked and see how long it takes for someone to make you cover yourself. Each society comes complete with their own set of stigmas.

We can't decide on walls either (ours are good, yours are bad). There are actually idiots out there that want to build a wall between America and Mexico! Forget for just a second the absolutely asinine logic that would have to be present in one's mind to think such a thing necessary, economically prudent or just. Didn't we just go through this with Berlin in the 80's? So, the country that was one of the biggest proponents of tearing that morally deplorable wall down wants to build one of their own? Well that's America for you, we can have walls, nukes and stupid laws about covering body parts but if another country does the same, they are a bunch of uneducated, fear mongering terrorists that must be stopped. Just for the record, did I miss the memo about ladders, shovels, boats and planes not existing anymore?

As Americans, we contradict ourselves by not wanting people to come to our country, and we use the term; illegally. That would mean that one would have to believe that "Americans" got here legally. By that logic, one would expect that as long as you invade our land, eliminate our people by whatever means necessary and make up a document declaring that the land that you "discovered" is yours, then you, my friend, are as legal as can be. And they say that the younger generation acts entitled. I'm not saying that they don't, but it looks like they might have just had really good teachers.

118

The government does it with seatbelts. If they say that they are worried about my safety I would have to ask, "then why am I allowed to juggle chainsaws, fire and knives"? If the argument is insurance rates, then only treat people that were wearing a seatbelt at the time or that have insurance, and don't help the person that wasn't wearing one and has no insurance. But to me, as crazy as it may seem, holding the right person accountable just seems right. They don't care about your safety, they care about invading your personal space and taking away your rights (executive directive 51, patriot act, USA freedom act).

Now, this being said, I think that the only thing more stupid than the seatbelt law is not wearing a seatbelt. You just don't have the right or reason to make me. Children, in contrast, should have to wear one until they are an adult and can make that decision for themselves. That is about the only seatbelt law that I wouldn't argue. Funnily enough though, I don't remember ever seeing a seatbelt in any of the school busses that I've been in, other than the one on the driver's seat. So, we worry about 1 unbuckled person in their hatchback on their way to work on a side street being a safety concern but not the bus full of kids doing 65 mph down the highway without 1 belt between them? Brilliant.

They do it with corporations and advertisement. Their willingness to not only allow, but also, to take part in littering our brains with ads, slogans and jingles implies that they think that these things are not adversely

119

affecting us. If this is the case then why do they not allow the tobacco companies to sell their product on tv and in magazines? I realize that, in the U.S., smoking is responsible for 18% of the preventable deaths, but obesity is responsible for 15% of them as well and I still see McDonalds commercials. You can see beer commercials while drinking a beer (alcohol) sitting on your couch (physical inactivity), eating candy bars and Doritos (poor diet), overweight like " literally" more than half of America and you are only 1 item (diabetes) away from doing all of the major causes of heart disease at once. Condoning and encouraging this behavior and allowing these other things to advertise at will makes me wonder who big smoking forgot to pay off.

 So, we've established that what is being condoned and allowed is not for your well-being, and is still being advertised. Then why the difference with tobacco? If ads don't have an effect on us, then why not allow them? If ads do have such an effect, then why allow all of the other deadly things to be advertised (cars, Doritos, beer, religion)? Why allow so many advertisements at all for that matter? Why not ostracize fat people like we do smokers? Why is shaming a smoker into quitting, or making remarks about how nasty and dirty of a habit it is, any different than telling a fat girl the same about her sandwich or her yoga pants? Where are all of the Truth ads about Twinkies? Being fat is way more pc than smoking is these days, but not a lot less dangerous.

Are you seeing the repetitious, double vision patterns replicating and repeating the redundant clones of the same idea again and again or over and over or again with this contradiction thing yet, or should I reiterate the recurrence?

 I find it odd that when the anti-gun nuts talk about gun control they don't ever argue to take the guns away from the police or the military. This says to me that they know that guns aren't the problem and that it is the people handling the gun that is the problem. This also tells me that they are not smart enough to know that the bodies that are wearing those uniforms are people too. This makes them just as capable of being unstable, vindictive, crazy and more than anything else as wrong as any other person. The point is, that it is the person, not the gun that is the problem and that logic should transfer to civilian life as well.

 As far as I am concerned, if those crazy, power hungry bastards (our government) are allowed to have fully automatic weapons and nukes, then I should be able to as well. If for nothing else, to be able to protect me and mine against them (read the 2nd amendment). Because they are not always right, I see them abuse their power and they should not be allowed to. That is why we aren't allowed to have those weapons, because they know that some of us would use them to take back what is ours. I would go further to say that this is probably the same argument from the countries that we won't allow to have nuclear weapons and I would have to agree with them.

121

Not that they should have them, but that we should not have them unless everyone else can as well. I see our fingerprints on more bodies that have died by nuclear hands than anyone else's. We are the ones that are sane? Have you seen our fucking president?!? Talk about contra dicting yourself.

This isn't to say that I do not support the individuals in our armed forces who adhere to the true values of right and wrong, have the best of intentions and stand fast for those beliefs even if it means not following orders. I absolutely do, when their efforts are not misguided by the agendas of the profiteers or even by their own twisted perception of right and wrong. Unfortunately, I believe that most of their honest efforts are being misguided by those agendas the majority of the time. It is a shame that, too often, so many of our young people die just for the rich to get richer rather than to actually "protect our freedom". I know that fights for our freedom do happen and I thank anyone that does, will or ever has taken part in them when that is truly what they are for. I support those troops and those troops only. If you're in it for the money, the prestige, to kill brown people or to follow orders no matter what, then you could not be farther from having my support.

We, as humans, contradict ourselves by constantly expanding and destroying everything in our natural world in the process. These are the things that are truly worth more than just money; the air, the land, our waterways, animals and oceans. Other things may be worth something, even a lot of something, but these things are worth everything and without them we'll have nothing. Still we can't ever get enough. Enough kids, enough cars, enough money, stuff or yards, it's just never enough. It's excessively sickening.

We are allowed to kill deer at a pretty staggering rate, but it's not because it is good to know where your meat comes from. It isn't so that you respect the animal more by taking part in ending its life for your sustenance either, but because there are too many of them and they are a nuisance. That sounds an awful lot like a species I know, but I'm pretty sure that they have thumbs. It's not as if the deer are taking fertility pills, getting drunk and hooking up, making land grabs and tearing your house down. That would be a nuisance, but does again sound somewhat familiar.

I think that Joe Rogan explained it the best when he called humans a, "very complicated form of bacteria". You can hear him expound on the topic by going to youtube and typing: Joe Rogan's theory on life and people. It's true, we are killing our host and we are expanding, just like cancer. We are going to run out of host at some point. There are people that are waking up to that fact now and the numbers are growing. Unfortunately, there are already forces that are entrenched, well-armed and stand to gain from its resources. These facts, accompanied by the entertained and the ignorant, are going to make it an uphill climb at the very least.

We in America profess to have freedom of religion, which I agree is more free than in some other countries. The lowest rung, however, is not the bar I am trying to clear. Freedom doesn't mean more free than most. The only bar I am concerned with is the one that says freedom, and you have to clear "that" bar to declare yourself free, not the marks of those who have failed.

How can you say that there is freedom of religion when children are made to say or even hear the pledge of allegiance with the word god in it (which didn't start until 1954), or be singled out? How could you then go even further and argue that the ten commandments should be anywhere near a school without fighting just as hard for other religion's rules to be displayed, or even want any displayed at all? How could you do that, and then hand your child money that has "in god we trust" printed on it (started in 1957) and say that there is freedom of religion?

These are generally the same people that happily or begrudgingly get behind whatever puppet is in office and goose step with the flock to kill people of a different color or belief. Whether they pull the trigger or just shout "mer!ka" from the couch, check-out line, tabernacle or hate rally, they are behind these killings "in the name of their god", their god who's sixth commandment is; thou shall not kill. Is this not the pinnacle of contradictions? Anyone that argues that wars are for anything other than profit has their hand in the ammo jar, is more blissfully unaware than a fairytale princess or should probably wear a helmet full-time. All wars are fought for Gold, Oil, Drugs and profits or god and prophets, it's really just semantics.

RACISM AND CHILI

Throughout this book I have been talking about how our choices separate us from each other. Obviously, some of the choices that separate us from some, end up connecting us with others. This is one of the ways that separation is good. If we didn't separate ourselves from each other in these multi-faceted ways, everyone would be the same and that is a world that I don't think I'd want to live in. If everyone thought the same way, dressed the same, talked and looked the same, it would not only be an uninteresting place, but we wouldn't have all of the different things that those many different thought patterns have invented. Transportation, housing, foods, medicine and electricity wouldn't exist and neither would any of their many forms. In any case, these differences are what give us the best chances for the survival of our species. Adversely, the refusal to accept those differences is likely to be what ensures our demise. Besides, if you don't get the design right like crocodiles, scorpions, horseshoe crabs, lampreys and the like, then you won't be around long enough to be but a blip on the evolutionary radar anyway.

 Separation isn't the problem at all, it is just another tool that we have at our disposal, and we get to decide how we use it. Again, the problem with things like flags, football, religion and separation in general is not the individual object or idea itself but the lack of acceptance. We are all different and that is a spectacular thing and until we can learn to accept those differences instead of demeaning others because of them, we are going to continue in this downward spiral. Separation is natural but doesn't always end badly and is not inherently bad. Division, on the other hand, may seem to help in certain instances but is not inherently good. Sometimes we decide to divide ourselves from a perceived problem. What happens when your perception was wrong and it wasn't a problem? What if you removed yourself from the situation, when staying and helping the problem would have helped you both? This is where a lot of the real problems begin. Division is separation with intent and these divisions are where fights, injustices and wars live. I believe that a lot of the division that we see is by the design of the wealthy and powerful in order to stay wealthy and powerful.

 Religion, flags, anthems, corporations and entertainment are all used as wedges to drive us apart and make us a less formidable opponent than we would've been together. This is not an opinion, but an observation that only the ignorant and blind cannot see. This is not to say that no good at all comes from these things. I realize that some good is done by these things and that some believers in these systems have good intentions, hearts and even actions. The problem with any of these things, as well as any other thing, is fanaticism. Fanatics can make anything dangerous because by definition it means to be obsessive and excessive. In general, it means unaccepting of others' beliefs, teams, thoughts etc., the need to convert others to their way of thinking and usually the willingness to fight about it, sometimes even to the death.

I even get the hypocrisy of my writing this book filled with my ideas and hoping that we're on the same page with most of them. This seems doubled by the fact that I will absolutely fight to the death for some of my beliefs (the important ones). I like to believe that the differences are that; I am not invading a village and forcing anyone to read this or telling you to believe it or die. As well, I am accepting of others' rights to these things as long as they aren't harming anyone. Also, the fact that the fight is only going to happen if you bring it to me or force me, with your actions, to bring it to you. Along with this, my mind is open to change, providing you bring valid, prudent, relevant and inevitably better information to the conversation.

You can dislike something without needing to condemn or destroy it. Take your least favorite food, spinach for example, just because you don't like it doesn't mean that it needs to be wiped off the face of the earth. You can just not eat it. You can even refuse to be in the same room with it, or avoid people that actually do enjoy the vile plant, that is your right. It stops being your right when you use your dislike for that thing to harm anyone in any way (providing we are still talking about spinach and not Hitler).

Acceptance of others' thoughts, rights and beliefs is crucial but also the acceptance that it may not be your job or purpose to go forcing these things on others. That means that you should be just as accepting of the gay couple down the street as they should be of the fact that their personal choice might not need a parade. Mostly if it causes children much too young for that conversation to have questions that they shouldn't yet be bothered with. You shouldn't expect to see a straight people parade either. You can be gay and be in a parade, you can be straight and do the same but neither of you deserves a parade in your honor like you are special because of your personal choice.

The same with religion, I am accepting of you having a "personal" relationship with a deity but why is it necessary for you to advertise that to anyone else or even speak of it in front of a child that will assuredly be changed by the thoughts of such things. It is, after all, a personal relationship, correct? Then why not deal with it personally? Children don't yet have the mental capacity to try to decipher the meaning of life or what sex is.

When they do, they should be exposed to the many different beliefs without being forced towards any.

I support your right to be what you want to be. There is an extent though, and I believe that there is for anyone. Otherwise there would be pedophilic, puppy choking, baby shaking parades. We have to limit that freedom at some point. When does it become a desensitization issue or a children's rights issue? That was not a rhetorical question, I would really like to hear the answer. It is fine if you want to juggle chainsaws, swords and fire, that is your right. It is not your right to do it around my children. If I want my kids to see that, then I can decide to take them to the circus. They may even see you doing it in your back yard and that is just as understandable. Granting all this, you don't have the right to do it in the middle of the street or a grocery store.

You are allowed to throw a loud concert, even of suspect subject matter, but not next door to my house. For that you'll need a permit and a place that can allow you to throw the event without trampling on everyone else's rights. This isn't anything against the music or the concert goers, it is just what is necessary to make sure that they aren't the only two parties whose rights are being protected.

People are born different. Some boys, some girls, some both. Some black, some blonde, some blind. Some with no limits, some with no thumbs, some with a tail. You are so lucky to be who you are and that is all that it is, blind dumb luck. You are no better than someone else because of who they are when they're born and you can't base your judgements of them on that. The choices that a person makes to separate themselves afterwards though, leaves them open to those judgements and they have to accept that. When judgements become actions, those actions inevitably infringe on the rights of the judged. This can't be accepted. Acceptance is also a tool that can easily be misused.

Racism is a tool that you have to wonder why we have at all. It seems like it can only be used for ignorant and evil purposes, yet as I've found so far in my life, any bad thing is a good thing for someone else. I have also learned that there aren't that many things that are of no use at all. The death of a loved one is one of the worst things that we can think of but the mortician, the pastor, the guy that makes the headstones, the flower lady and even the worms get to eat because of it. They wouldn't get to pay their mortgage, send their kids to college or buy a new boat (maybe not the worms) without it.

I have a hard time finding the good point for racism. It does have different degrees, from historic preservation of culture to decimation of other races and I can't find the intelligence in either argument or any in between that I've heard. It is difficult trying to find the positive that would have made it a trait worth our brains keeping. I came up with the only reason that I can even think of it existing at all.

Let me preface this with the facts that I am not a doctor or a political scientist, nor do I practice or condone racism. I will love you or hate you no matter what color you are. My judgements are based on actions, not skin tones. I don't care about color, belief, law or popular opinion, I care about right.

In this instance I am going to use dogs as an example again. A mutt dog generally tends to be, overall, healthier than a purebred as far as genetic diseases are concerned. This is the case because we don't keep mixing up the gene pool of the purebred as much and just like a password, if you don't change it frequently you give hackers the time to work on it. In the purebred's case the hackers are diseases like hip dysplasia that dogs like Rottweilers and German shepherds and other large breeds are prone to. This is not to say that a mutt will never have hip dysplasia but that the chances are much higher in those pure breeds.

Much like a mutt dog, I believe we are much healthier, if not more interesting, when we mix our ideas, cultures and races. It is beautiful to watch yellow and blue mix to make green but if you continue to do that with all of the paints on the palette then you just get this gray brown blob. Having used all of the paints to make these colors, you don't have the ability to change that blob's color by using any of the original colors.

Look at it like a pot of chili. You start off with separate piles of tomatoes, beef, beans, onions and spices on a cutting board. You put some of all of these ingredients in to the pot to make your chili (mixed people). Now when anyone gets a bowl of chili, they can throw in some extra beans or onions from one of the piles left on the cutting board and the chili can always be different. When I think of the piles of ingredients I see them as races and in the middle of each pile are a few pieces of beef, onion or bean that refuses to go into that pot. That one little tomato in the middle that doesn't want his kid mixing with that bean down the street. That piece of beef that can't even stand the smell of an onion let alone the thought of mingling with one.

As you get farther away from the less exposed and therefore less educated center of the pile, you find that even though they might not want to get in the pot, they are more likely to hang out together on the cutting board and even genuinely enjoy each other. This is mixing at its best, everybody gets what they want. When the onions invade the tomatoes, though, things will never be the same. You can't get that smell out of anything and now there are so few tomatoes that don't smell like onions that you might as well put them off to the side in a reservation dish.

If you take the cutting board and dump all of the ingredients into the pot you lose the ability to make each person's serving different. You have also lost the ability to change the pot of chili because you have no individual ingredients remaining. Now that pot of chili is just a pure breed mutt. No more mixing up the gene pool. Disease is bound to find its way in, even if it's just in the form of thought. If we don't have different ways of thinking and solving problems then we are bound to find a problem that we cannot solve.

In this respect, and this respect only, can I find reasoning in my human brain for such a heinously barbaric tool. It looks as if racism is evolutionarily necessary for our survival. It isn't pretty and I don't like it at all but I view death in pretty much the same way. It's not at all a desirable thought but it is inevitable and necessary for the survival of the whole. It isn't a pretty sight to watch a lion feed on a water buffalo's entrails as the buffalo writhes and moans in pain. But the lion isn't being violent because of its upbringing or because it played too many video games. This is nature and just like earthquakes, tornadoes, hurricanes and the fiery collisions that we observe creating planets, it doesn't have to be pretty to be the way that things are supposed to be. I don't agree with racism but I don't agree with people dying from a tsunami either. I also don't get a choice of whether it is supposed to happen or not. All you can do is try your best, put up your best defense and hope that it's good enough.

We have to accept the onions and the spices towards the outside of the piles (as long as they aren't trying to wipe our pile off of the board). We have to oppose the beans and the beef in the middle of the piles that would have beef only be with beef and beans with beans so that they stay few enough in numbers not to be a serious threat to dinners everywhere. But I think for the chili's sake we have to leave a little bit of the middle of all of those piles on the board. That way everybody gets to eat what they want (as long as you want chili).

 I may very well be wrong and again want to express my distaste for this idiotic practice. I think racism is bullshit and that the ignorant degenerates that don't think so, regardless of color, have issues that their meager intelligence and faulty moral compass will probably never overcome, but thunder doesn't always mean rain. Sure gets you looking at the sky though.

 Anyone that thinks that they are of pure descent is fooling themselves, which makes them the fool. Even the colors of the visible spectrum are made of different wavelengths or frequencies that have to react with other particles to exist, making themselves not even purely one thing. These base frequencies mix with each other and with other elements in our atmosphere to make even more variations of those colors. The color that you perceive an object to be is actually only the reflection of the only colors that the object cannot absorb. Black is not even a color at all, but an absence of light because it absorbs light and can't reflect the colors contained in it back to your eye. It's funny that some of the people most proud of their "white" color being pure, associate themselves with something that by scientific definition is actually not a "color" either, or pure. It is the reflection of a mix of all of the colors of the spectrum. It is a fairly accurate comparison when concerning their acceptance (absorption) of colors though, isn't it? If color or even light aren't pure, how could one expect that their lowly human form is?

Religion, school and even life, to a certain degree, are kind of like a stencil that the teacher gives the students. Everybody gets the same cutout and choice of decorations but the projects all look very different by the end of the class. Some students will use different colors but even when they do, there is still the variable of the application of those colors. Some will be very neat and tidy while others will get outside of the lines and be messy. Some will decorate with glitter, macaroni or marshmallows and some with all of them. Some will only use it as a guideline or as part of an abstract design. The choices are as varied as the minds that orchestrate the creations.

We do the same thing when we are handed that stencil of school, religion, life and even the information that we encounter. We all have our own take on what it should be, based on our original self and our experiences. We will all decorate them differently because of this and because of the many variations of ornamentation that each individual picks up along the way. This is why it's not the Christians, Muslims, politicians, athletes, universities, individual races or other countries that anger me. It is the individual and their interpretation of that stencil and how they decide to decorate it.

It isn't the stencil of the Christian religion that bothers me so much as it is the individual that decides to decorate it with their own twisted vision of adornment.

Rather than use the compassion, forgiveness and generosity that their "faith" calls for, they use pride, greed and gluttony in their place and call themselves virtuous. It is not the stencil of the Muslim faith (Islam), it is the people that contort its book's verses or color extremely outside of the lines with mediums such as violence and terrorism that their book strictly and blatantly admonishes. Calling either message more evil or violent than the other just proves ignorance (both say some horrible and beautiful things). The same can't be said for the follower's interpretations of said message. Those need to be taken into account individually as does most everything. It is the people that practice the opposite of what their faith preaches but still claim that religion that give the people that do adhere to its values a bad name.

We have the issue, in America, with Islam that I'm sure they have with Christianity. Ignorance, propaganda and extremist fucktards keep people fighting and building walls instead of learning and truly connecting. I would argue that these people are not Christians or Muslims, but rather that it's just what they call themselves. I can call myself a woman as much as I want but if I stand up to pee, don't bleed once a month and don't have a uterus then I'm not really a woman, I'm just calling myself one. I must admit, I would be bringing down the curve to say the very least (as are the false "believers").

My feelings are the same for any individual and the stencils that they carry with them. I don't care what school, belief or race stencil that you have, I care about how you choose to decorate it and where and how you choose to display it. You can embellish it as ornately or as slovenly as you like in your own home providing that it isn't harming anyone but yourself. The problem comes when you feel the need to force your design on others by putting it on their house or forcing them to comply with your vision. By doing this, you're not allowing them to enjoy their stencils or elaborations with the same freedom that you expect to be granted to yours.

Equality has to be equal or you have to call it something else.

#chilirocks

THOUGHTS AND CLOSING

To wrap things up, separation is inevitable, integral, fundamental, good and bad. Just like any other thing it can be used to help and to harm. Decisions that were made for us, and the choices we decide to make for ourselves, make us who we are. They are what help to make every single person on this planet different. Those differences are what make this life exciting, joyous and worth living. Or, as Michael Franti said, "all the freaky people make the beauty of the world". Appreciate the differences and indulge in the splendor that they can provide.

We need to be accepting of each other's differences (like the color orange) and realize that just because someone else believes something doesn't mean that we have to. The same goes for the other side of that coin. Just because someone doesn't like the same thing that you do, doesn't mean that they need to be converted. Acceptance is absolutely the key to the solution but it is a very hard thing to do. Not for the easy stuff like paint colors or potato chips, those are easy enough to accept. The hard things like nationalistic, ethnocentric, xenophobic and religious ideals are the places that acceptance is the hardest to apply. We need to accept the fact that just because something is different or even offensive to us doesn't mean that it is wrong. However, when it infringes on your rights, it is wrong and should not be accepted.

We need first to understand what our rights are. They are not given to you by a piece of paper, or someone's imaginary friend. They are yours because you are a living thing. Secondly, we must understand that if we have them, then so does everything else and that those rights should be considered equally. That means that the plants, animals and even the soil have rights. We do not have a right to the land and all of its bounties at all costs. To quote an ancient American Indian proverb, " We do not inherit the earth from our ancestors. We borrow it from our children". This couldn't be more true, yet we strip, mine, pollute and outright devastate it in every corner of the globe with little to no concern of the wellbeing of future generations. This is unacceptable and far from our right. Land is an earthling's right, not just the right of those who can afford it.

You do not have the right to force your religion on someone else. This is the same for the individual believer as it is for the pope or the government. You do not have the right to poison someone's mind with fabricated fallacies and xenophobic agendas. You do not have the right to express yourself just because someone else does. You do have the right to express yourself to an extent. You have the right to brand your face, tattoo your eyeballs, have sex with who you want (providing they're consenting and legal), root for and pray to whoever you want but if it means stabbing puppies and kicking them down main street, you don't have the right to express yourself in that way.

 In the same way, if it may be traumatizing to a child or cause conversations that should not be had by a child, then you don't have a right to have a parade about it. That goes for everything from gay pride to white power to Christianity. You don't have a talk with your 3-year-old about sex for these very reasons. If you do, you probably shouldn't be allowed around your 3-year-old.

 The right to believe the way that you want to believe is what you want, correct? Just remember that it is what "you" want and that your child deserves that same right as well, so don't take it away from them by forcing your beliefs on them. They are called yours for a reason. Let them keep that right to their belief, and just hope or pray (or both) that they will be as kind to their children.

 Acceptance at all cost is not acceptable and there are always going to have to be limits on what is acceptable. Not all people are good and if there aren't limits, then the people that aren't, and sometimes even the people that think they are, will take advantage. It goes back to that most basic of tools; greed. For this very reason, I believe that we will be our own undoing whether that be by war, pollution, over population or decimation of resources. Part of me is sorrowful for the ones that wouldn't have seen it all wasted, and other parts of me feel as if it is deserving. Some of us have made our bed and others are content to sleep in one that was made for them but both are equally as deserving of such a fate. Whether you are the perpetrator or the one that sat idly by while it happened and entertained yourself, instead, with something else like American idol, the big game or god's word, you are all at fault.

 Every person has a right to freedom but that freedom isn't free, you must fight for it at every turn. You must be vigilant and informed, which is hard to do if you care more about who the Kardashians are dating or whether your running boards match your mud flaps than you do about the shitty choices of politicians you are being given. I tend to agree with Jax's dad, "people don't want the freedom to be free, they want the freedom to be comfortable". Comfortable is great but not at someone else's expense, not even your own.

 It isn't the tv, video games, drugs, guns, money, power, greed, flags, football or religion that are the problem. It is the misuse and abuse of all of these things and more that is a problem. It is a lack of accountability, personal responsibility, compassion, acceptance and above all, parenting. We as parents need to compassionately accept that it is our personal responsibility to be held accountable and to try to help find solutions rather than create problems.

Be accepting of people's differences and unaccepting of those who aren't. Help those in need and even those who are not whenever you can. Do these things for those people, for future generations and for the good of mankind, not for your own ego or the praises of others. Seek love in every beautiful meadow and every dark alley and help to grow that love. I believe it is just as necessary to extinguish evil as vehemently as you seek that love. The only problem with that is that my definition of evil may differ from yours.

Fighting will never end. We as a species have been doing it since we got here and you can look around nature and see that we are not the only ones fighting. We are however the most powerful, vicious, detrimental, rapacious killers to inhabit this planet. We and housecats are, after all, the only things on this planet that kill for fun (the cat thing is our fault too). All we can do is try to truly love our fellow man and the earth that sustains our life, as well as be understanding, compassionate and to work towards these goals for the betterment of humanity.

The hope is that by educating and caring for each other, that we can compete with the numbers of those who don't have our best interests in mind. Together is the only way that we can win this war. Divided by languages, flags, gods and colors, we make ourselves easy targets for those that would look to keep us slaves. Make no mistake, if you let them continue to do things in your name, if you patriotically do their dirty work for them, if you keep killing for a god that condemns the act, if you blindly pledge your allegiance to something that shows no allegiance to you, then a slave is exactly what you are. Be a slave to the grind of compassion and critical thinking instead and we may just be able to tip the scales in our favor.

Everybody isn't on the same page as anybody and they won't ever be (because we are people). It is one of the reasons that I don't know if we will ever "fix" this world (or if we're supposed to). I do think that we can unfuck it a good bit by wanting and trying to understand each other better. This starts by realizing that different doesn't necessarily mean bad. As alike as someone may seem to you, they still have their differences and as different as someone is, they still have their similarities. These are both cases for celebration rather than vilification. Even if you don't agree with the particular difference, the fact of difference being an option is just as worth celebrating as finding that similarity where you didn't expect.

Stop believing the hype and getting caught up in it, because they will sell you that shit till you're broke. Expect more from "your" government, you are the people that it is for and by, and in the end, it is your representative to the world. Don't settle for such poor choices and demand punishment and replacement for those that would give them to you. It is your government, not theirs, start treating it that way.

I know that sometimes you may feel alone, as if there is nothing you can do and that the odds may seem insurmountable. There are others out there though, and their numbers are growing. Be that as it may, we seem severely outnumbered by the ones that are too dim to see the light or that would hope to douse our flame. At times it can feel as if you're trying to light the world with a handful of matches, but remember, it only takes a spark. Just a spark to start a fire that demands recognition, that can't be ignored and that, once large enough, can consume the largest and most twisted forests (problems between races, religions, ideas). If that's the case, then a handful of matches should be more than enough. Even if it isn't, you can still be that spark, and set this world ablaze.

Quit super sizing everything! We get it, you have a small penis (or tits). Being morbidly obese and driving a hummer on steroids to your house in the burbs doesn't make it any bigger. Try not to want as much. Try to think about people that haven't had a meal in days. If you need to want, then want to love, want to care, want to inspire. Stop worrying about the newest phone, nicest car and designer clothes. Start worrying about people that don't have a home or that just feel alone, because they are unfortunately abundant and can be found in your country and even in your city, no matter where you live. Treat the person in another country or city with the same respect and dignity that you and every other human being deserves, until they prove that they don't deserve it. And don't judge them by their leaders, at least half of the people (in most cases more) are not happy that it is their leader. How could you ever expect the same in return if not? Stop keeping people out and start letting people in.

Travel around and see the spectacular wonders that this gorgeous planet has to offer. Talk to strangers, get addicted to love, don't stop learning and don't be afraid to dream. Remember, life can sometimes get in the way of your dreams but it is just as important to make sure that your dreams don't get in the way of your life. Don't try to be better than someone else, just be the best you that you can possibly be. I think that there are few words to live by that sum it up as eloquently or succinctly as the ones used when Satchel Paige said to, "work like you don't need the money, love like you've never been hurt and dance like nobody's watching". The only thing that I would add is that you should apply the last part to everything in your life. Live it, in its entirety, as though no one is watching, which I like to think, is what he meant by it anyway.

If I would have gotten as in depth as each of these topics would require to feel fully covered, this book would have no end. I urge you to take it upon yourself to research (from multiple sources) any of the things in this book, as well as your daily life, that you question or wonder, be it for more information or in search of its validity. There is a wealth of knowledge, questions, bands and ideas waiting to be discovered in the reference section. Do yourself a favor and look through it before you pass this book along to someone else that wants to know how flags, football and religion have fucked the world. Because the fanaticism of these things (and things like them) surely have.

This is a poem from 2005 that led to my decision to write this book. I don't think it's great but it is the book's predecessor and I thought it deserved recognition of at least that.

AWAKE

You can lead a sheep to water
And he'll drink up all you've got
Even the Kool-aid, fuck, mostly the Kool-aid
Anything to keep from original thought
Their favorite flavor is buy me
Or the one that they see the most
It didn't really happen if it wasn't on tv,
In the times or in the post
Oh please give me something to buy
I'll believe you when you say, "they were brought down by things that fly"
Just tell me a story, because most will believe
That those who do not are the ones misconceived
And hell yes, we will let our young die and bleed
Even though instead of freedom, that oily shit tastes like greed
And when we find out that it was what it is and it is what it was

And that they died for your book, thought or some made up cause
We'll just give you more kids and money
And say, kids, he has flaws
But what's that on the roof honey?
Might it be Santa Claus?
Or maybe some other thing I once said was true
Who cares about truth boy?
My dad told me, so I'm telling you
So go ahead, lap it up, like your mom, dad and friends do
Do you really think the shepherd would let anything dirty get through?
I mean, I know we are sheared and cut up for meat
But people need to be warm and even wolves need to eat
And I know that the shit in our pens comes up past our feet
But maybe it's the fluoride or cancer or Teflon
Or being told, "they're your neighbor, but they are for being told on"
Or maybe it's the sitcoms and football I'm sold on
I don't really know, but I know we must hold on
To this dream, this matrix or picturesque illusion
To think for ourselves would cause mass confusion
Delirium, chaos, at the very least, delusions
Some of grandeur, freedom, peace love and hope
Who the hell are these hippies? They must all be on dope
Or hopped up on something because you can't possibly think

That the government would put anything bad in your drink

Or shit in the air that causes legions, tumors and worse

Or that they worship the devil while cloaked, chanting verse?

Because they're the ones we elected, right? Maybe not

But then again, that brings me back to thought

And my time for that, I've got not a lot

Because the game's on and my wife wants to show me the shoes she just bought.

And after that, I don't know what I'll do

But whatever it is, it won't be with you

Because you may get killed next for what you say, think or believe

And if I'm seen with you, I might get it too

Who cares, we can't change things, we are but a few

I mean, I know a few others, and they know a few more

But there couldn't possibly be anything that we few can do

Because that would take time from my busy schedule

And I still have to wash my new car

And didn't you say that rally's in D.C.?

Isn't that just a little too far?

Cause gas is real high now, and I don't get paid much

And there's not much left after iPhones and such

But I really wanted one because all the cool people have them

And I need to get email and listen to tunes

And to have pics of my stuff and scores, hope we beat 'em
Is it just me, or do you smell those fumes?
I thought this train was taking us for a weekend with the sky
This doesn't look like any camp I've ever seen
And who the fuck is this F.E.M.A guy?
What's with all the barbed wire?
And who are the guys with the guns in the jeep?
I guess they must be protecting us son,
Let's just go back to sleep

THANKS AND STUFF

I want to thank any of you that actually managed to make it this far, for suffering through this journey. I would also like to thank the ones that just flipped through it, straight to the back, and are reading these words, for doing even just that. I do look forward to hearing your feedback and am excited for the conversations, information and relationships that I hope to be a by-product of this effort. I hope beyond hope that we can somehow right this sinking ship. I meet people quite often that re-affirm my belief that there is hope, as bleak as it may seem at times. The bad news is that they are outnumbered by the copious amounts of stupid, brainwashed, comfortable puppets. The good news is that "We, the people that give a shit" (my next book), have decency, intelligence, compassion, what is right and love on our side. I adore these weapons but we can't ever forget about the deadly weapons that our adversaries possess. Being loving, vigilant, informed and willing to do what is necessary should be your main concerns if we are to prevail. I am going to end with an oldie but a goodie just because it's too true not to, so please remember; we may not have it all together, but together we can have it all. Follow me on Twitter @BrodieMacLean2 and let's start a conversation we can learn from.

Thanks again!

QUOTES AND SAYINGS

The Grateful Dead – Sometimes you get shown the light in the strangest places if you look at it right. (3)

Unknown – Religion is like a penis. It is fine for you to have one and even to be proud of it but don't take it out in public, don't force it on children, don't force it down other's throats, don't make laws with it and don't think with it. (5)

Wookiefoot – If love is not the answer then we just asked the wrong question. (5)

Bruce Lee – Empty your mind, be formless, shapeless like water. If you put water into a cup, it becomes the cup. You put water into a bottle, it becomes the bottle. You put it in a teapot and it becomes the teapot. Now water can flow, or it can crash. Be water, my friend. (5)

George Orwell – Happiness can only happen through acceptance. (6)

Ram Daas – If you think you're free, then you can't escape. (7)

Dr. Seuss – Be who you are and say what you feel because the people that mind don't matter, and the people that matter don't mind. (7)

Joe Rogan – People are a complicated form of bacteria. (8)

Jax's dad (sons of anarchy) – People don't want the freedom to be free. They want the freedom to be comfortable. (10)

Michael Franti – All the freaky people make the beauty of the world. (10)

Ancient American Indian proverb – We do not inherit the earth from our ancestors. We borrow it from our children. (10)

Satchel Paige – Work like you don't need the money, love like you've never been hurt and dance like nobody's watching. (10)

Unknown – we may not have it all together but together we can have it all (thanks and stuff)

GLOSSARY

addiction – a state of being given up to some habit, practice or pursuit.

arpeggio – the notes of a chord played in succession, either ascending or descending.

bolstered – support or strengthen; prop up

cataclysm – a large scale and violent event in the natural world

chauvinistic – feeling or displaying exaggerated patriotism. Excessive or prejudiced support for one's own cause, group or sex.

despotism – the rule of a despot; the exercise of absolute authority and control.

disease – a disorder of function in a human, animal or plant, especially one that affects a specific location and is not simply a direct result of injury.

devoid – entirely lacking or free from.

devout – having or showing deep religious feeling or commitment drug – a medicine or other substance which has a physiological effect when ingested or otherwise introduced into the body.

elaboration – the process of developing or presenting a theory, policy or system in further detail.

ethnocentric – evaluating other people and cultures according to the standards of one's own country

fanatic – a person filled with excessive and single-minded zeal, especially for an extreme religion or political cause.

fascism – a political philosophy, movement or regime that exalts nation and often race above the individua land that stands for a centralized autocratic government headed by a dictatorial leader, severe economic and social regimentation, and forcible opposition.

freedom – the power or right to act, speak or think as one wants without hindrance or restraint.

holocaust – destruction or slaughter on a mass scale, especially caused by fire or nuclear war.

idiosyncrasy – a distinctive or peculiar feature or characteristic of a place or thing.

intrinsically – in an essential or natural way.

Marxism – the political and economic theories of Karl Marx and Friedrich Engles, later developed by their followers to form the basis for the theory and practice of communism.

nationalism – patriotic feeling, principles or efforts. An extreme form of this, especially marked by a feeling of superiority over other countries.

omnipotent – (of a deity) having unlimited power, able to do anything.

Oriental – of, from or characteristic of Eastern Asia.

patriotism – vigorous support for one's country.

plethora – a large or excessive amount of something.

prevalent – widespread in a particular area at a particular time.

privy – sharing in the knowledge of (something secret or private)

propaganda – information, especially of a biased or misleading nature, used to promote or publicize a particular political cause or point of view.

slovenly – messy and dirty (especially of a person or their appearance)

touted – attempt to sell, typically by pestering people in an aggressive or bold manner.

xenophobia – intense or irrational dislike or fear of people from other countries.

Some of these bands are political, some emanate positivity, some of them just jam but they are definitely all worth checking out.

BANDS:

Wookiefoot

Michael Franti and Spearhead

Useful Jenkins

Immortal technique

Cult of the Flag

Rage against the machine

Corporate Avenger

Palehorse

Groovatron

Spookie Daly Pride

Michael Kelsey

Shpongle

Animals as Leaders

Dirtfoot

Keller Williams

Split lip Rayfield

Tauk

Andy Frasco & the U.N.

VIDEOS:

Constitution class – Michael Badnarik (7 – 1hr classes)

Empire of the city (world superstate) ring of power

America: Freedom to Fascism

Theft by Deception – deciphering the federal income tax

Monopoly men

The money masters

In debt we trust

Money as debt

Zeitgeist

Truth and lies of 9/11

9/11 Press for truth

The story of stuff

Pirates and emperors

Who killed the electric car

The illusion of reality

Spin

Philosophy, physics, mathematics – Dangerous knowledge

What the bleep do we know? – Down the rabbit hole

Lost lightning: The missing secrets of Nikola Tesla

Aldous Huxley – Gravity of light

The future of food

The world according to Monsanto

The root of all evil

The century of self

The doctor, the depleted uranium and the dying children

Dark secrets: Inside Bohemian Grove

Evidence of revision

JFK II – the Bush connection

The Mena connection

Waco – A new revelation

Ruby Ridge

These videos can be found easily by using google or youtube. I highly suggest checking all of them out but keep my earlier advice in mind when you do; believe everything from no one. Take notes and research the things that you have questions about.

MOVIES:

Network

V for vendetta

Steal this movie

Idiocracy

Wag the dog

What plants talk about

SLC Punk

Pay it Forward

The American ruling class

PODCASTS:

Joe Rogan experience

The Brilliant idiots

Otherhood

Dan Carlin's hardcore history

Capitalisn't

The Daily Zeitgeist

BrainStuff

Higherside chats

Ron Paul Liberty Report

Stuff to blow your mind

BOOKS AND WRITINGS:

The United States Constitution

The Declaration of Independence – Thomas Jefferson

Behold a pale horse – William Cooper

1984 – George Orwell

Animal farm - George Orwell

Brave new world – Aldous Huxley

Be here now – Ram Daas

A man without a country – Kurt Vonegut

1776 The year of illusion – Thomas J. Flemming

Dupont – Behind the nylon curtain – Gerard Colby

Lies my teacher told me: Everything your American history textbook got wrong – James W. Loewen

True hallucinations – Terence Mckenna

Dmt: The spirit molecule – Dr. Rick Strassman

Lies the government told you – Judge Andrew P. Napolitano

What is property? – Pierre-Joseph Proudhon

End the fed – Ron Paul

The Revolution: A Manifesto – Ron Paul

The school revolution – Ron Paul

God, No! – Penn Jillette

The Bible

The Quran

Sutta Pitaka

Thanks to Tracey, Roger, Josh, Jeanne, A.B., Lisa, Rob and Eric for the reads and opinions. The book wouldn't have been the same without you.